"I read this all through tonight and blessed all together. The fir unfinished in my mind. I am stitutions become self-preserving very quickly and deprive individuals of their personal value in the process."

> – **Paul de Neui,** *Professor of Missiology at North Park Seminary*

"Phenomenal. Should transcend Christian / secular divide."

> – **Soong-Chan Rah,** *Professor of Evangelism at Fuller Seminary*

"I met Neil Taylor soon after becoming President of the Evangelical Covenant Church in 1986. He was a key leader in bringing the JPUSA community into the official membership of our denomination. It was a Christian commune of several hundred persons living together in the slums North Side of Chicago. Over the years he and I became close partners in common mission on behalf of the poor. He and his wife Pegge have influenced my life as have few others. Loving and gentle, he has complete faith and integrity. He led JPUSA through dramatic miracles and suffering. This is his incomparable story."

> – **Paul Emanuel Larsen,** *President Emeritus of the Evangelical Covenant Church (1986-1998)*

"I just finished the book. Yours is one of those extraordinary lives lived in relative anonymity, observed only by your family and close friends. Reading the book reminded me just how much I treasure our friendship."

> – **Tom Cameron**

"I just finished reading your story last night. Though I was familiar with much of the story, there was additional info and clarity shared that helped me understand and feel like I was living it along with you. Well written and compelling."

– John Herrin

"In 1829 Edgar Allen Poe penned a poem in which he compared our lives to a trail that we essentially walk alone. He eloquently describes how our lives soon become a rich odyssey that defines us as others start to walk beside us. Some for a short time, some for a long time. Some we wish would have stayed longer while Others we secretly wish would have departed much sooner. At some point however we realize the sun will soon be setting on our journey and we'll find ourselves reminiscing in the quiet recesses of our minds where only we go. Only a few of those special companions that became part of our lives will come to mind, while the majority remain buried in the sands of time. The precious souls we do recall are invariably those who profoundly impacted our lives and shaped us into the person we became.

"I encourage you to allow this author to join you on your trail of life. His example and inimitable life course in the selfless service of others will influence you profoundly. One day when you realize that the inevitable concluding epoch of your journey has arrived you will recall the name Neil Taylor and most assuredly fondly recognize the impact his story had on you."

– Tim Schmadeke

The Great Unfixables

11/1/2022

To Dick & Deb

Golfing friends at Pacific Springs.

Galatians 6:9

Neil Taylor

The Great Unfixables

A Memoir

What I Learned From 45 Years
In a Christian Commune

Neil Taylor

atmosphere press

– Dedication –

I write for my grandson, Max. I hope one day he comes to see the Mystery at work in his Pop's life and will open himself up to the Mystery to be at work in his. Yes, I want him to know that through all the messiness of life he can encounter a God who loves him and desires to be his friend. Someone once told me, "I don't pray for my children to know God. I pray for them to experience God." My prayer for Max is to "taste and see that the Lord is good." (Psalms 34:8).

I write for my family: my wife, Pegge, and daughters, Mindy and Kirsten, who experienced the varied joys and sorrows I have, whether they wanted to or not. They know my stories, so I seek to preserve the stories for them. I hope it encourages them to reflect on their own stories, which are far more valuable than mine because they are theirs.

And, last but not least, I write for the community where I lived the longest part of my life here on earth. I love and care for all those with whom I lived and served with for over forty-five years. They will always be close to my heart and remain at the center of my prayers.

"In the end, we will remember not the words of our enemies, but the silence of our friends."

– *Martin Luther King Jr.*

– Foreword –

I cannot now remember when I first met Neil Taylor. Perhaps we crossed paths before I came to North Park Theological Seminary as president and dean. But early in my presidency at North Park I do remember him preaching in the seminary chapel. I was struck by his modesty and his honesty about the struggles of forming and sustaining an intentional Christian community like Jesus People USA. I still remember him telling the students and faculty that, when asked for advice about forming such a community, he would respond that he could not tell the questioners *how* to do it, but he could certainly tell them what *not* to do given that Jesus People had made every mistake in the book! Our friendship was really launched when I began to work with the pastoral staff at Jesus People to prepare them for ordination in the Evangelical Covenant Church. I was closely involved in a series of classes specially developed for their benefit. I was moved by the intelligence, thoughtfulness, and commitment of that group. Over the following years I became much more familiar with Jesus People through my participation in the late, lamented Cornerstone Festival, through teaching and preaching at Jesus People, and through my developing relationship with Neil. The tragic death of a troubled Covenant pastor who had come to Jesus People after the collapse of his life and ministry took our friendship to another level. For several years, we met regularly for lunch and spiritual conversations. Those are treasured times and I look back on them with deep gratitude.

Neil is one of the most genuinely visionary leaders I have ever met. To develop and sustain a community like Jesus People, one must be both visionary and tough-minded, collegial and flexible. Jesus People drew troubled and wounded people to the community. Its leaders came to understand that many of those wounds were not easily healed, and some members of the community could wreak havoc without intending to do so. This required discipline and courage on the part of the leadership. It required setting boundaries and enforcing rules—something human beings are, to say the least, not always happy with. In my experience, Neil demonstrated the kind of tough-minded compassion that was necessary for such a community to survive. Neil, along with the other members of the JPUSA leadership team, also demonstrated an ongoing desire to learn and grow intellectually as well as spiritually. This was seen in the many famous teachers and scholars they invited to address the community and the ways as individuals they pursued further learning. In Neil's case, this meant pursuing a deep interest in Spiritual Direction —an interest that continues to motivate him and enable his growth and ministry.

Over the years, I heard many of the stories you will read in the following pages—but not all. When Neil sent me the manuscript, I read it in one sitting, enthralled by the narrative of a privileged, confused, and desperate young man who found an unlikely family and life's work with a motley group of "Jesus freaks." But I also lived through perhaps the most painful part of the story with Neil. As you will read, I was at his side when the church and community he had so ably served called him to account for some ludicrous charges that stained his reputation and radically altered his life—charges the leadership of the church was finally forced to acknowledge to their humiliation were untrue. I was frankly astounded by how badly both the church and the Jesus People community mismanaged the incident. It still makes my blood boil. I am no longer a pastor in the Evangelical Covenant Church. While the treatment of Neil was not the principal reason I chose to resign my ordination standing, it was certainly a contributing factor. But all of this is Neil's story to tell, not mine. And he tells it well.

Neil and I still speak once a month. He keeps up with my life in retirement in Minnesota and I keep up on his life in Omaha with his beloved wife Pegge and with his adventures with his grandson Max. I consider him one of my dearest friends, a man of integrity, courage, and hope. He has in recent years taken many blows, wounds given in the house of his friends, as the Scripture puts it, and endured. This is the story of a man of God who was involved in one of the most important movements of the twentieth century and a member of one of the most successful and vibrant ministries of outreach and compassion of that era. His life and ministry will continue to bear fruit, and I trust that we will continue to share life and ministry together. I also hope that by telling his story he will not only speak truth to power but find healing and peace. I further hope those "friends" who wounded him will be able to face their complicity and failures and seek reconciliation and offer restitution. But whatever the case, Neil's legacy is secure and rich in friendship and accomplishment.

   – John E. Phelan, Jr.
Emeritus President and Dean
of North Park Theological Seminary

John E. Phelan, Jr. retired as Senior Professor of Theological Studies at North Park Theological Seminary. There he taught courses that ranged from introductory New Testament and Worship courses to seminars on Eschatology, the Gospel of Mark, and the poet and novelist Wendell Berry. For fourteen years he was president and dean of the seminary. His PhD is from Northwestern University/Garrett Evangelical Theological Seminary. He served as a pastor of churches in Florida and Kansas.

– Preface –

Three people come to mind who have encouraged me to write. They're all friends, though I wonder whether anyone who encourages you to write a book can be called a friend. Either they don't like you, or they're crazy enough to think you have something to say.

One of those friends is a political journalist, Mick Dumke. Mick has written for several publications: *The Reader, The Sun-Times, The Chicago Reporter,* and *Pro-Publica Illinois.* One of Mick's claims to fame was provoking Mayor Richard Daley by questioning him about the effectiveness of gun control in the city, and having the mayor respond with a threat about wishing to shoot a gun up Mick's butt. Is Mick a pain in the ass? Evidently, the Mayor thought so, but that hasn't been my experience with him.

Mick and I became acquainted twenty years ago as regulars at the early morning lap swim at Chicago's Gill Park district pool. Mick was finishing his education at McCormick Seminary while holding down a job, eventually finding himself in a failing marriage. I was pastoring a large intentional Christian community located in the Uptown neighborhood of Chicago, navigating daily life with its nearly three hundred members as my wife and I grappled with our youngest daughter's life-threatening addictions. There was something life-giving about our brief exchanges over the temperature of the water or whatever stresses we were experiencing at the time. Putting our heads under the water gave us a momentary sense that we had escaped our painful realities as we were being surrounded and held by something larger than ourselves.

Eventually, Mick and I began meeting for breakfast once a month, allowing us more time to air our complaints in the hope of experiencing a greater measure of God's all-surrounding grace. One morning at the Original Pancake House on the corner of Clark and Armitage, Mick said, "Have you written down your stories? You must start."

Another voice urging me to write was that of a man I only knew for a couple of weeks before he committed suicide. Terry was a Covenant pastor who had lost his family and his church. After a year or more of extensive therapy, I received a phone call from someone in my denomination asking if Terry could come and stay with us in our community. When he arrived, I helped settle him in a room. I had planned to put him in a room shared with two other men, but upon inspection, the room was, to put it mildly, rather untidy. I put him in a much nicer room, one he could have to himself. It was far more comfortable, clean, and private. I still wonder if I should have put him in the messier room with the others.

Terry and I spent time in the evenings drinking decaffeinated tea talking about our lives. He spent each day serving meals at the homeless shelter our community operated. His gentle pastoral presence was felt and appreciated both by the homeless and the staff at the shelter. Terry was profoundly gifted in showing compassion for those in need, but the loss of his family and church weighed heavily on him, more than anyone knew.

I was out of town for the weekend when I received the phone call informing me that Terry had taken his life. Our community held a memorial service for this man we had only known for two short weeks. It was astounding how much he had left his imprint upon all who met him, especially me. Terry left a farewell note beside his bed, and in it he bequeathed to me a Balmain fountain pen in an ivory leather case. Terry wrote, *Please give this pen to Neil and tell him to write his story.* That was more than ten years ago, and now the pen has found its way out of my desk drawer and sits beside my keyboard as I type. I look forward so much to renewing my friendship with Terry in heaven one day.

Lastly, I had the good fortune of meeting Jean Vanier in the early 1980s after reading his book, *Community and Growth.* Jean was the founder of L'Arche, a worldwide community-based outreach for people with disabilities. A friend let me know that he was giving an open lecture at the University of Illinois. After Jean spoke, I invited him to come for dinner and see the community where I lived. To my surprise, he accepted. After dinner, I drove Jean back to his lodging and volunteered to be his chauffeur whenever he was in the Chicago area.

Jean would become my mentor and friend. He came often to Chicago over the next few decades, once bringing the L'Arche U.S. leadership team to our home for a spaghetti dinner. The typical routine when he visited was to eat dinner with the eight pastors of our community and afterward address the community members at large. He'd often begin by saying, "We all know life in community is a horrible reality! Some are okay, but the others, pffft!" Everyone would burst out laughing, knowing the bald truth of what he was saying. Once the laughter died down he would add, "But it is a place of our growth. Jesus is here." We were all intimately aware of the grace it took to practice patience and love towards each other. Without Jesus, it would be impossible.

It was obvious how much I was influenced by Jean Vanier. I had read all of his books and would regularly reference some insight of his. Someone said to me after a sermon I'd given, "Congratulations. You did not quote Jean Vanier once in your sermon this morning." My response was, "I apologize. It won't happen again."

I visited Jean's residence in France in May 2017. For an entire week, Jean and I shared meals in one of the L'Arche homes, the Val Fleury. Every day we'd take a stroll through the little village of Trosly-Breuil. While walking one afternoon, Jean commissioned me to write a book about my life in the community. He said, on three separate occasions, "I want two hundred pages from you." I couldn't help but think of the talk between Jesus and Peter at the end of the gospel of John when Jesus asked Peter three times if he loved Him.

I wonder if I have fulfilled the wishes of these three friends. Mick marveled at the many curious stories I shared about finding my way through the stresses of pastoring and living in community with others. Terry, whom I only knew for a brief amount of time, wanted me to write about finding a second chance in life, something he couldn't find for himself. Jean wanted me to share about what life was like in my community.

The inspiration for this book doesn't come only from

these three friends but from all the people in my community with whom I shared life together for nearly fifty years. Living and learning in their presence was the most profound experience of my life.

– Chapter One –
Miscarriage of Justice

The hotel I'd chosen was in a section of town that wasn't the most desirable. I didn't realize that when I made the reservation. I had been told to come to a meeting with the Board of the Ordered Ministry of the Evangelical Covenant Church and to bring a support person. I brought my friend, Jay Phelan. He never complained about the poor accommodations. If I had been told that our expenses would be covered, we would have stayed at the hotel where the meeting was to take place in downtown Detroit. But, with limited income, it's second nature for me to look for the best deal.

I didn't sleep well on the roll-away bed. In the middle of the night, it sounded like cars were drag-racing right outside our door. It felt like we had narrowly escaped our room being broken into and robbed, so it was a relief to check out early the next morning and make the rest of the trip into the city.

People greeted us outside the meeting room as if what I would face was no big deal. In fact, that's exactly what some people said. "Oh, don't worry. I've been suspended before, too." If it was no big deal, then why was I being asked to attend this meeting in the first place? Everyone who knew me seemed to agree that the situation that brought me here was a complete error of judgment from the outset. I breathed deep, trying to relax as Jay and I headed into the room. This wasn't my first rodeo with this board, but I'd always been in the role Jay was in, as the support person.

The meeting began with polite introductions from the twenty or so people gathered there. I was familiar with about half of those on the board, but some I'd never met. Most everyone knew the community I was a part of, and some had even visited for a week or long weekend to help us serve the homeless in the shelter we ran. Nonetheless, I began by sharing about my decision as a young, eighteen-year-old kid to join a fledgling community of twenty-five people, where I remained as a member for forty-five years, where I married and raised my two daughters, and served as a co-pastor with seven others for over forty years.

Eventually, I got around to the story that was being told about me, charges that had never been raised toward me throughout my entire history in the community. I shared the fantastical details of the allegation and the history of the person who had made them. Jay and I were asked to leave the room while everyone on the board came to a decision about my future. When we were invited to return, what seemed like hours had been, in reality, only about forty minutes. A letter of resolution from the board was read aloud.

In the end, it felt like I had been invited to attend the meeting in order to go through the proper protocol, and my history of faithfulness accounted for nothing. The decision had already been made. My suspension was upheld. I could not preach or teach in any Covenant church and had to leave the church I pastored.

I was invited to remain seated while everyone in the room gathered around to pray for me. One person said, "This is a kind of Joseph situation for you." Of course, I was familiar with the story of Joseph, and who in the world isn't after Tim Rice's Broadway musical *Joseph and the Amazing Technicolor Dreamcoat*? But if I was Joseph, what role did the board play in the story? Certainly not Jacob, the brokenhearted father of his absent son thought to be dead. Perhaps the mean-spirited, jealous brothers who cast Joseph into a well and decided ultimately to sell him as a slave?

This was all too much to process. I didn't react with any emotion because I must have been numb or in a state of denial. Little did I know that the board's decision would be the beginning of a miscarriage of justice that would result in a complete termination, uprooting my sense of calling and all that was familiar to me.

– Chapter Two –
Wanted and Loved

I was a wanted child.

My sister was born first, in May 1951, but I believe my dad was looking forward to having a namesake. When I came along three years later, I was given his name and became Neil Christopher Taylor Junior. My sister was given my mother's first name, Janice, but not her middle name, which was Olive. My mother was very thin and used to be called Olive Oil by her classmates. With two Jans and two Neils in the same house, a considerable amount of time was spent clarifying who was being called. My younger brother, Mark, had an easier time being identified.

When I was young, I didn't like my name either. Classmates made up rhymes with it, like "Neil, Neil, the banana peel," and "Get real, Neil!" and "What's the deal, Neil?" On top of it all, I attended a parochial school where my name was announced every morning in the chapel service by the priest saying, "Let us kneel." I could sense my classmates staring at me. I tried telling others my name was Jimmy, but it never stuck. Thank God others named Neil found popularity in the sixties, such as Neil Armstrong, Neil Diamond, and Neil Young. By the time Neil Patrick Harris became popular, I was beyond disliking my name. To this day friends still make up rhymes with my name. One is fond of calling me "Neil shmeel." But now, at sixty-seven years old, I find it endearing.

—

Not long after I was born, my parents discovered something was not quite right with me. They'd often discover fresh blood on my sheets and in my diaper. When I was three my mother told the doctor she knew something was wrong because of how large I was around my midriff. Two weeks later, I underwent a splenectomy at the Baptist Hospital and was diagnosed with a congenital disorder referred to as portal vein thrombosis. The result of this condition is often an enlarged spleen and internal varicose veins lining the esophagus wall. The enlarged veins can burst without warning, leading to internal hemorrhaging. At one point, my parents were told that it was likely I would not live through my teens. Years later, in my twenties, when I was still dealing with unexpected hemorrhaging, a nurse who became familiar with my medical history said, "Your poor mother." Until I had my own children, I did not appreciate the fear my parents must have lived through.

The child who was wanted and welcomed into the world became the child who required special care. Are parents ever prepared to deal with a child with special needs, or do they find grace in the moment to rise to those responsibilities? Having a child who could bleed to death without warning must have been harrowing, but neither of them flagged for a moment in providing care for me. I was extremely fortunate to have such special people as my parents.

My fragile health was likely more difficult for my dad, who had always been athletic and looked forward to me stepping into his shoes. All contact sports were off-limits for me, but nonetheless, my dad's competitive spirit lived strong within me. I would undergo four life-threatening surgeries before I was thirty and survive them all. My dad used to say when I was young, "You're the toughest little guy I've ever known." He was a wimp when it came to doctors. I was the opposite. My dad was an attorney and, as such, became an aggressive advocate for my healthcare. He was present for every surgery, even when I got older. His presence was like a prowling lion on every hospital wing I was on, demanding attentive care by all doctors and nurses. He made Shirley McClaine in *Terms of Endearment* look even-tempered.

Not long ago, by chance, I was paired with two doctors at a golf course in Omaha. Over the course of eighteen holes, I shared my unique medical history with them. One of them commented off-handedly, "You're lucky to be alive." The other was completely baffled about how the diagnosis was made about my condition since the necessary imaging technology wasn't available at that time. My story must have taken their minds off their game because I ended up with the low score for the round.

It's often said, "Life is an uphill battle." Despite having so much privilege in my life, I am, nonetheless, intimately acquainted with the uphill climb of it all. Someone once asked me what I would call a book if I wrote one. What came to mind was, *I Lived*. Did I have a choice in the matter? Sort of, and I continue to choose it; that is, I continue to live it. My experience has been that the uphill parts of my life were not merely difficult, but were also the places I made the greatest discoveries about myself. All of my life lessons have been built on that first truth: I was born into a world where others wanted and loved me.

I wonder how I ever came to the point of believing the opposite.

– Chapter Three –
I Feel Sick

When I was in fifth grade, I awoke in the middle of the night with extreme nausea. As I made my way into the bathroom of our Florida ranch-style house, I instinctively checked the dirty clothes cabinet behind the door—a habit I had developed after a family outing to see the movie *Psycho*.

After inspecting it to make sure Anthony Perkins wasn't hiding there, I braced my hand against the tile wall to ease myself down as I proceeded to pass out. My head must have hit the floor with a thud that woke my mom, who would wake at the drop of a feather. I regained consciousness with my head in her lap. I barely got the words "I feel sick" out of my mouth before I vomited a stomach full of bright red blood across the yellow tiled floor. My mom yelled for my dad who, hearing the alarm in her voice, sprang out of bed straight into his pants. Moments later, I was in my dad's arms being carried to the car. He had to wave off our dog, who growled instinctively in an attempt to protect me, and soon we were speeding towards the Baptist Hospital. No time was ever wasted calling for an ambulance when I was hemorrhaging.

Earlier that day, I had run track at my school, Grace Chapel Episcopal. It was the first day our school used the running track at Bolles Academy right across the street. I spent the next week with my arm strapped to a board with a sterile metal needle inserted into a vein as I watched one endless bag of blood after another drip into my body. Transfusions up to that point had been successful in stopping the hemorrhaging, but my parents were advised to take me to a specialist at a children's hospital in Columbus, Ohio. The surgeon there was considered the leading expert in the country on my condition. By doing a small exploratory surgery, he could determine if I was a candidate for another surgery that might extend my life.

I wasn't told beforehand why we were going to Columbus and cried when I discovered I was going to be admitted to a hospital. The surgeon was Nigerian, with blue-black skin. I didn't think of my family as being racist, but black people where I lived were the yardmen, maids, or caddies on the golf course. When the yardmen came to mow the lawn, I would spend the day outside playing among them. It never crossed my mind to question why there was a separate bathroom in the garage for them, or why most of the black people lived in one particular area in Jacksonville, on St. Augustine Road and Emerson, a place I was told to never ride my bike through.

The nurse who attended to me while I was in Ohio was African-American. She and I became buddies right away. She liked to give me a hard time, and I gave it right back. Her name was Nurse Wagner, but I called her "Wagon the Dragon."

The exploratory surgery determined that the second surgery would not be possible. As far as I was concerned, that was good news. Before we left to head back home, my parents invited my nurse, Wagon the Dragon, to come to visit us in Florida. I've never forgotten her response: "One thing my mother always taught me from the time I was young was, 'Honey, don't go to hell, and never go South.'"

—

In the summer after seventh grade, my family went on a water-skiing vacation at Lake Lanier in South Carolina. When you drove down the mountain from the lake you were in a little town called Tryon, North Carolina. The vacation started with a long day of water skiing and being bounced around on an inner tube at high speeds behind the boat. I awoke the following morning feeling sick to my stomach. I let my mother know I wasn't feeling well and didn't want any breakfast.

Trying to coax me into feeling better, she said, "Maybe we'll have to take you to see a doctor."

She had barely stepped out of the room before I spewed fresh blood all over the white-painted deck floor of the boathouse. My dad was nearby so he scooped me into his arms and ran up the hill to the car. My aunt, looking out the window and having no idea what had happened, called the hospital to let them know we were coming. Both of my grandmothers flew into the nearby town of Spartanburg, South Carolina to be present with me and my parents in case this was the big one. I was able to see them just before I was rolled in for surgery.

As it happened, the surgeon-in-chief at this hospital in the little town of Tryon was one of the ten on-call doctors to President Lyndon B. Johnson. Had it not been for the skillful hands of Dr. William Bosein, I doubt I would have survived. The surgery took eight hours. He was able to find the burst vein and tie it off. I was left with a scar that wraps from the middle of my abdomen halfway across my back. Basically, I was cut in half and afterward felt like I'd been run over by a Mack truck. The road to recovery was long, and when school started that September I still looked frightfully thin and pale. A schoolmate said to me, "It would have been cool to have a friend who died." It's crazy how that kind of thoughtless juvenile remark can remain embedded even fifty years later. The person is now a Facebook friend. I've never reminded her about what she said, and believe she would be completely unaware of having said it.

That surgery prolonged my life. It would not be until I was in my twenties that the hemorrhaging would begin again.

– Chapter Four –
The Incomparable Mamma

Growing up with a possible terminal illness had its advantages. When my parents said no to something, I'd call my grandmother. Comedian Sam Levenson said, "The reason grandparents and grandchildren get along so well is that they have a common enemy." Mamma was always my best ally. My four-and-a-half-year-old grandson is already mastering some of my adolescent skills. My daughter tells me that when things aren't going the way he wants, he announces to both his parents, "Call Pops!"

Mamma, my dad's mother, was a working woman. Her typing and shorthand skills kept her employed during the Great Depression. Today she may have been considered an essential worker. When my dad was six, Mamma became a single working mother. Family folklore recalls that she would give my grandfather some money every day to go in search of a job. When she discovered that he was squandering it on wine and women, her oldest brother, my great-uncle Neil, and his two brothers ran my grandfather off.

"That's how things were done at that time," he later told me.

Mamma was Catholic, so she never remarried. She had one child of her own but also raised her two nieces with the help of her mother, my Great Grandmother Belle. My only memory of my Great Grandmother Belle was when she died. I must have been about four years old and was told not to go into the spare bedroom of the house. But, when no one was looking, I peeked inside. There on the bed lay my Great Grandmother Belle fully dressed but no longer breathing. I quickly shut the door and, of course, never told anyone what I'd seen.

Mamma was as faithful and trustworthy of a person as you'd ever find. One day, when she arrived at work, she was told that money was discovered missing from the till. She was accused of stealing and was fired. She felt humiliated and distressed. Later that night, the owner of the company called her to say he knew she was innocent and that it was his son who had stolen the money. He begged her to come back, but the experience was so upsetting for her she chose not to return. Afterward, she was hired by an older couple who owned a cemetery in Jacksonville. Oaklawn was hailed as the South's most naturally beautiful cemetery, with its giant oak trees draped with Spanish moss. The cemetery was advertised in film reels that played in theaters before a movie. Mamma became more than a secretary to the couple, who had no children of their own, by caring for them and taking them to their doctor appointments. When they died they left her everything—their house, their business, their wealth—along with some debt. I was told she had to sell a box of their jewelry to pay off the taxes. This inheritance gave her the means to send my dad to law school.

As a kid, I spent a lot of time with my grandmother. Everyone needs to be someone's favorite, and I believed I was hers. For one thing, I was her son's namesake.

Mamma's pet name for me was Big Ears because she said nothing passed by my ears unheard. One of the things I overheard was that her first child was stillborn, which may have endeared me to her all the more, considering I too was at risk for an early death. My sister Jan and my younger brother Mark would also believe they were her favorite. Perhaps that was Mamma's gift. She could make everyone feel special.

For me, the cemetery wasn't a place of ghosts and spirits of the dead. It was a huge playground with lots of things to explore. One grave marker was a life-sized statue of a lion that I loved to sit on. I was told the man was a lion tamer all his life. I never did ask how he died.

Whenever anyone came into the cemetery office, Mamma would send me to the back part where there was an old Underwood typewriter waiting for paper to be scrolled in, with keys that quickly got stuck together. There was also a large safe, big enough to crawl into, making me feel like I was the valuable treasure inside. Mamma's last words to me when she sent me to the back were always to be very quiet while she met with people who were dealing with the loss of a loved one.

Once a woman came in to make funeral arrangements for her mother. As Mamma was helping her with the burial plans, it became clear that the woman had a sister who was not present. Mamma had enough experience with the possible tensions that can arise with funerals and said to the woman, "It's important for your sister to be part of the planning."

The woman shot back, "I have not spoken to my sister for ten years."

Mamma replied, "Then think how happy it would

make your mother to know that her daughters reconciled upon her death. I suggest you call your sister and invite her to come here with you, and then we can complete the plans."

The woman stormed out at my grandmother's suggestion, planning to take her business elsewhere. She returned a few days later and said, "I called my sister as you suggested, and neither of us could remember why we stopped talking to each other."

—

The cemetery was more than a business to my grandmother. It was her mission, her calling. There was no one better to talk with than Mamma when you faced a crisis. I knew that better than anyone.

After school one afternoon, I was riding my bike through my neighborhood looking for my dog, Popeye, a Boston Bulldog who unfortunately loved to chase cars and bikes. I passed a couple of older girls in my neighborhood on their bikes.

"We're sorry to hear about your dog," they said. I knew they were saying my dog had been killed.

I said, "Thanks," and pedaled home as fast as I could to explode in tears. I called Mamma at her office, barely able to talk. She already knew that Popeye had been run over, but listened through my hysteria and eventually said, "Well, you can be assured Popeye is not suffering or in any pain, and in time you'll get another dog. But knowing how special Popeye was, we can find a place out here at the cemetery to bury him."

Popeye was buried near the garages where the trucks

and equipment were stored. The hole had already been dug by the cemetery men by the time we brought Popeye later that same day.

—

Mamma did not like frogs. Uncle Robert, one of Mamma's brothers, had a voice that sounded like a bullfrog from too much drinking and smoking. He used to catch giant bullfrogs and put them in a bucket under his house for me. I spent a lot of time digging big holes in my backyard for frogs to jump through, much to my father's chagrin. For school, I did a science experiment of a volcano erupting lava. I had some leftover granules of the flammable substance I'd used for the volcano demonstration, so I made a small mound of it on the cement patio outside in my backyard, creating a little ring of fire. I placed a small frog in the middle of the ring, expecting it to jump over the fire ring. It stayed put and burned to a crisp. Not long after, my grandmother picked up the phone at work to hear me sobbing as I recounted the tragedy.

She said, "Honey, you didn't mean to harm the little frog, and the frog is not suffering."

The frog didn't get a formal burial like Popeye did. The cemetery didn't allow cremation burials at that time.

—

One of my favorite pastimes was frequenting the pet store on Beach Boulevard. This pet store had unusual things besides dogs, cats, birds, and goldfish. One day while I was there with Mamma, I discovered, to my great surprise, a small alligator for sale in a little terrarium typically reserved for turtles. Later that afternoon, I walked into my house gleefully carrying my new pet alligator.

The store owner had explained to my grandmother how to clean the terrarium, so Mamma proceeded to tell my mother how to do it. "Janice, you just catch the alligator by the back of its neck in order to rinse out the terrarium and add fresh water to it."

My mother looked at my grandmother and said, "Leonora, whenever it needs cleaning, I'll call you to come pick up that alligator."

I built a little pen for it in the backyard next to our house. I liked to spray it with water from the hose, so I could see it open its pink mouth. One day the alligator was gone, leaving my mother to fear that someday a ten-foot alligator was going to crawl out from under the house.

In truth, my mother was also a softie when it came to animals. While shopping at a J.M. Field's department store, my brother Mark and I headed straight to our two favorite sections: toys and pets. The pet section mostly had the typical department store collection of birds and goldfish, but that day, as we wandered the aisle, we discovered a baby spider monkey for sale for thirty-five dollars. We ran with all our might to find our mom and both of us, out of breath, exclaimed, "We promise to be good for the rest of our lives if we can get this one thing!"

"What is it?" she asked.

"You have to come see for yourself."

I've always thought the nearest my parents came to divorcing was when my dad came home that evening from the law office to discover a caged baby monkey in the laundry room staring up at him. My dad insisted the monkey be checked by our vet, who called later to say he had never seen such a healthy monkey.

Maxwell Smart Taylor lived with us for a year. He had an outdoor cage about six feet tall. If you've ever visited a monkey house at a zoo you know how strong an odor monkeys have. Whenever we left the house in the evenings, I believed my dad would go and unlock the outdoor cage, hoping the monkey would run away. But Maxwell Smart Taylor knew a good situation when he had it, and when we arrived home, he would be hanging on to the doorknob, waiting to get inside. While we were at school, my mom would feed Max fruit cocktail along with his bananas. Maxwell figured out how to untie the twine of his cage indoors and would make a beeline to my mom, who was oftentimes standing at the sink preparing dinner. It was common to hear a scream of surprise when his little hands grasped her leg to climb up. More than a few dishes hit the ceiling.

Spider monkeys get big, so after a year, we donated him to the Jacksonville zoo. We were told he would be happier there, and my dad promised that we could have two picks of our dog's litter in place of the monkey. We had the puppies for two weeks before my dad became impatient with housebreaking them and they went to new homes, too.

The other strange pet we had was a coatimundi. My little brother Mark had to have it. It lived outside in a cage near the garbage cans. I believe more than one family moved out of the neighborhood due to us Taylor children.

To me, we were a typical family, but how can a kid compare his family with others? In *Leave it to Beaver*, Beaver was always causing some kind of mischief, and we weren't much different. Tempers flared at times, but no one was ever hit or smacked around, which isn't to say spankings were non-existent. At family gatherings, my brother Mark often said, "I got a spanking every day." My parents would laugh and, of course, deny this.

Vulgar swearing was never heard in our home, but we knew my mother had reached her limit whenever she said, "Hell's bells!" Occasionally, she'd also say, in utter exasperation, "Someone, please, call the nuthouse. You kids are driving me batty!"

Being a smart aleck, I often shouted back, "What's the number?" as I reached to take the phone off the hook.

– Chapter Five –
It's All Been Paid For

When my brother and I would leave the house to play, my mother would always yell out the door after us, "Don't go down to the river."

"Yes ma'am," we'd say out of respect, but usually that was exactly where we were going. There was a twenty-foot bluff with roots sticking out for us to climb down and multiple sandbars to be explored. I lost many shoes stepping into the foot-deep mud on the banks of the St. Johns River. There was a fishing hole on a little creek feeding into the St. Johns where we'd sink waterproof explosives and watch the shocked fish float up to the surface. We often saw snakes on the banks but, fortunately, no alligators, though they can be seen.

Mamma's house in San Marco was across the street from an inlet of the river. She tried to instill fear in me by saying there was sinking grass in the pond. It worked. I had seen episodes of *Tarzan* where people were swallowed by quicksand, so I stayed clear of those waters, which in truth were filled with nothing but seaweed.

Mamma was not the stereotypical Southern grandma known for being a good cook. Since my mother had taught me how to scramble eggs, that was my job whenever I stayed over with Mamma. The secret to making good scrambled eggs is cooking them over low heat and taking them off the burner just before they're done. Mamma's job was to boil water for the grits and make toast. Mamma did make some mean coarse grits that had to be soaked overnight, and it was only at her house that I enjoyed guava jelly on my toast.

Many mornings we ate out, and some of the most important life lessons I ever learned came during those times. We often frequented a little diner two blocks away from her house called the Hastee Tastee. Ida Smith owned the restaurant, and Ida adored me. She and her boyfriend took me deep-sea fishing a couple of times on their yacht.

One of the waitresses was an older, thin lady who had one of those deep smoker voices. She never seemed to have much to smile about, and I would have never guessed that she was happy to see us, or anyone for that matter. Mamma ordered her usual poached eggs, extra brown toast, and a cup of coffee. Since she always ordered her toast extra brown I assumed that all older people liked everything to be near burnt and crunchy. As for me, it was always the same: French toast, bacon, and a small glass of orange juice. Mamma always added a glass of milk for me to drink, also.

One morning, the grumpy waitress brought Mamma her coffee in a cup that was cracked. Mamma mentioned it to the waitress and asked for a different cup. A couple of minutes later another cup of coffee was served, but the second cup also had a crack in it. Mamma had a phobia about drinking out of a cracked cup. She believed germs lived in the cracks, so she could not enjoy her morning coffee out of a cup that was cracked. When the grouchy waitress came back, Mamma apologetically said the new cup also had a crack in it. When the third cup came with a crack in it, Mamma told the waitress she would do without any coffee.

My French toast came grilled to perfection. There were four half-slices stacked across the plate with a little ball of melting butter and powdered sugar sprinkled on top. I made sure that my French toast was swimming in syrup so that some got on the bacon, too.

After breakfast, when it came time to pay the bill, Mamma did not leave the waitress a tip. We left and drove straight to the cemetery office. When lunchtime came, Mamma said she needed to go back to the Hastee Tastee because she felt bad over the exchange with the grouchy waitress. Mamma had concluded that it was partly her fault for having the phobia in the first place.

When we got there, Mamma asked Ida if she could speak with the waitress who had waited on us that morning. There was a look of dread on the woman's face when she saw my grandmother standing by the cash register. She stood quietly in front of us and her employer, waiting for what she must have thought was going to be a dressing down. Instead, Mamma said, "I did not leave a tip for you this morning, so I came back to give it to you. I realized it is not your fault that I have a phobia about drinking out of a cracked cup. I apologize and wanted to bring you your tip." Mamma reached out and handed the woman a dollar bill.

The grouchy waitress began to tear up and said, "No, Miss Taylor. It was all my fault. I felt so embarrassed that I brought you coffee three times in a cracked cup. How could I have been so stupid?" The waitress and Mamma became good friends. They knew each other by name.

From then on, whenever my grandmother and I went there for breakfast, she always made it a point to wait on us. She actually seemed happy to see us. One thing was sure, she never served coffee to my grandmother in a cup that was cracked.

Mamma and I also shared many meals at the Lakewood Pharmacy, which was two blocks from the cemetery. It was common in the 50s and 60s for pharmacies to have a restaurant or soda fountain. The Lakewood Pharmacy had a long winding counter with little green stools and matching green vinyl-topped tables with green chairs. When I was with my grandmother, we always sat at a table. When we were handed our menus, Mamma would say, without fail, as if it was part of her religion, "Now order whatever you want." But I always ordered the same thing: a patty melt, which was served open-face on a piece of buttery toast (not rye), French fries, and a vanilla shake. Mamma liked liver and onions, a meal I would not learn to appreciate until many years later.

One day, while waiting for our food, two boys came in and pulled out all the change in their pockets. They placed it on the counter for the waitress to help them count it. They were hoping for two chocolate milkshakes, but the waitress, seeing that they didn't have enough for shakes, suggested two cherry Cokes.

When the waitress brought us our food, Mamma quietly asked the waitress to get the two boys each a cheeseburger, fries, and a large chocolate shake, saying, of course, she would pay for it. The two boys must have wondered why it took so long for their two cherry Cokes to come. When the waitress put down the two cheeseburgers, fries, and chocolate shakes in front of them, I don't know if the look on their faces was delight or fear. The waitress gave them a big smile and announced, "It has all been paid for." Leave it to Mamma to be way ahead of the curve of paying it forward.

I never bothered to tell anyone this story, not even my parents, because this was simply who Mamma was. She never let an opportunity to be kind pass her by. Little did I know at the time, but this event would be recalled to mind ten years later when I, too, would come up short-changed, although in a far greater way than the two boys at the counter that day.

– Chapter Six –

Howie in the Hills

When I was in second grade, I began learning Spanish. I made A's in the class after the first year because we kept re-learning the same thing—how to count to ten, say our names, and ask "Como esta usted?" By fifth grade, I began to ask my parents if I could be a foreign exchange student to a Spanish-speaking country so I could become fluent, but my health issues were a non-starter. Eventually, years later, the closest plan I could come up with was to go to a boarding school for the summer. I finally succeeded after tenth grade to convince my parents to let me go a couple of hours away from Jacksonville to a school near Orlando. I was eager to complete some extra courses, and I was motivated by something else, as well. I wanted to distance myself from friends who were experimenting with drugs, and I was looking to distance myself from some foolish decisions I'd made.

I had my learner's permit, so my parents let me drive the three of us to Howie-in-the-Hills Academy. On the way, I lit up a cigarette and, with one hand on the steering wheel, said, "You might as well know I smoke. This is part of the reason I'm going away, to try to put aside all my bad habits and improve my life."

Both of my parents smoked, so although they were

surprised, they could hardly protest.

Despite my desire to leave bad influences behind, I soon learned that many of the kids at the academy were spoiled brats from well-off families whose parents were off-loading them for the summer. It wasn't my parents, but rather me, trying to off-load myself, but it would prove to be harder than I thought. I wasn't in my dorm for five minutes before one of my roommates said, "Did you bring any cigarettes?"

I pulled out my pack and handed it to him. Being familiar with the thoroughness of room inspections, he unscrewed the air-conditioning vent near the ceiling to hide the cigarettes in the ductwork. By week two, a girl and I were caught smoking in a nearby cornfield. Punishments were called "sticks." A stick was a small slip of paper put in your mailbox outlining the crime and the punishment. A copy was sent to your parents.

My punishment was to work in the kitchen six hours a day for a week. At breakfast, I made toast for everyone on a conveyor belt toaster. When the toast came out, I used a paint brush to spread melted butter on each piece. Every now and then I would just dunk the whole piece in the vat of butter.

When summer school ended, I managed to complete two courses that I wouldn't have to take during my junior and senior years of high school. I didn't have a kind of *Breakfast Club* ending where some of life's problems found resolution. My lofty hopes of improving my life were not realized at all. If anything, I left more discouraged about my own inability to straighten out my life, and my sense of aloneness was all the more present. Driven by my insatiable desire for acceptance, I tried to outdo others by taking whatever new drug became available. No doubt about it, I was cool—I mean, a fool.

One night, a friend's parents had gone to their beach home, which left their in-town house empty. Four of us decided to try a new drug that was available. Not knowing how strong the drug would be or its effects, it was similar to playing Russian roulette. I only have vague memories of the night and am unclear whether the memories are real or not. Someone recounted to me that I peed on the front door of one of the neighbor's houses. My friend Lisa and I were out of our minds. Fortunately, a person with us who was not as affected drove us both to my house in my car and dropped us off with my parents. On the drive there, I took off my shirt and poured an entire bottle of coconut oil all over myself. When my parents came to retrieve me from the car, I must have looked crazed, glistening from head to toe. I could not be coaxed to get out of the car until my mother said, "Look, Charlie got out of the house and needs you to get him back inside." I jumped out, grabbed my dog, and went in.

Lisa's dad was a doctor. He drove back into town from the beach and gave us both a shot of a sedative to calm us down. When he approached his daughter, who was sitting on my mother's lap, she hit my mother on the head as she tried to escape the hypodermic needle in her dad's hand. Maybe she thought her father was trying to shoot her up with heroin. I must have showered and was lying naked on my bed when Lisa's dad came to give me mine.

The next morning, I was sitting at the breakfast table drinking a glass of orange juice when my dad came in and said, "Do you want to talk about it?"

I said, "Talk about what?"

He explained enough for me to start remembering pieces of the previous evening's drama.

I told him, "You don't know what you're talking about."

He replied, "No. You don't know what you're talking about."

He left the kitchen. I opened the back door and discovered my car parked in the garage in my mother's spot. I think my parents were hiding it because we had caused enough of a stir in the neighborhood that the police had been called.

My dad came to my high school the following Monday to take me out for lunch. He spoke with the dean about what had happened. The dean came into my classroom, announced my name, and told me to step into the hallway.

"Your dad has come to take you to lunch," he said. "I don't think you realize how lucky you are to have a dad like you do."

At lunch, my dad and I discussed trying to do things together. I convinced him that what we needed was a ski boat to help bring us together. Soon after, I got a ski boat. We may have skied a couple of times, but in the end, the boat became a great place for me and others to party.

How deep can ingratitude run? It certainly ran deep in me. I never doubted whether or not my dad loved me, but the deeper, unanswered question was, "Does my dad like me?" This question would resurface many years later, when my brother, Mark, mentioned he wasn't sure if Dad liked him or not.

I was never the sports enthusiast my dad must have hoped for. I preferred learning to cook with my mom. The first cake I made had to have the icing poured on top of it like syrup. I thought two-thirds of a cup of water meant two to three cups of water. I mastered making chocolate chip cookies, each with a half pecan on the top, because my mother believed in putting nuts in everything.

It was always easier for me to relate to my female cousins, easier for me than for my sister, who was more their age. If a girl could be described as a Tom-boy, I was the opposite. I didn't have words for it at the time, but I was haunted by questions about my own sexual identity. Every time I came home from a hospital stay looking deathly pale, I'd sneak into my mother's makeup drawer to add color to my complexion. Anything to make myself look healthier. As I got older, I spent as much time in the sun as possible. Perhaps like every kid, I loved exploring woods, climbing trees, and spending lots of time down by the river banks catching tadpoles. I was athletic in the sports I could participate in, and was always picked to be captain of whatever team games we played at recess. I had a group of guy friends who I hung out with at the local country club, where we gambled and paid our debts with our parents' charge accounts. One of my friends lost a Surf and Turf dinner to me on the putting green. When his dad reviewed the month's charges, my friend's spending privileges were revoked for a month.

I did alright with the girls, too. In grammar school, a classmate came back from the restroom to tell me there were two girls from the public school outside wanting to see me. They had the day off and had come to my school to flirt with me. In high school, I was elected to be the mascot of a girl's club. I had "knock-out" girlfriends. Yet, by my senior year in high school, I also had sexual experiences with three male friends. I was plagued with questions about my own sense of normalcy or, perhaps better put, what I believed to be "abnormalcy."

About that time, I began having a persistent desire that haunted me day and night. I wanted to start my life all over again. In the mornings, I'd look into my bathroom mirror and see a crazy person. I found myself repeating aloud what a close friend often said to me: "You're mental." She meant it as a joke, but I took it seriously.

I tried commanding myself in the mirror to, "Be happy." But nothing I said made my life any different. I would spend hours driving around in my new Camaro with no place to go and no one to hang out with. The isolation and loneliness were suffocating. I exhausted myself trying to change who I was, and my efforts seemed to only make matters worse, hurling me into greater despair.

One day, in the summer of 1971, some classmates showed up at the San Jose Country Club, where I worked as a lifeguard. My family belonged to four country clubs. Some classmates of mine had just returned from a week-long youth retreat in the Rockies with a group called Young Life. They shared how deeply moving the week had been, and I sensed their genuine excitement about their experience.

One of them said, "We couldn't help but think how much you would have liked being there."

I shrugged and said, "I doubt I would have been interested." I headed back to my lifeguard stand to bake in the sun. I had a momentary feeling that I had missed out and secretly wished someone would have encouraged me to go.

I got high as often as I could to escape my loneliness.

Once, I ingested a drug early in the evening but did not feel the effects until I got home later. I sat in bed, unable to fall asleep. Perhaps hallucinating, I began imagining myself going back in time, one year at a time, to see if I could identify which door I must have gone through to have ended up in the miserable place I was in. I was awake for hours, never finding the door, or maybe discovering there were too many. In my eight years of daily chapel services in my Episcopal grade school, I was taught to pray on my knees. So I crawled out of bed and knelt down to pray. My prayer was stark and straightforward: "God, if you can change my life, You can have it. Amen."

At that moment, I sensed a quiet whisper in my heart. I heard the words the waitress had said to the two boys at the drugstore counter ten years earlier as she set the burgers, fries, and milkshakes in front of them. "It has all been paid for."

I wish I could say something tremendous followed that message, but I crawled back into bed and slept soundly as only a teenager can. I was awakened by my mother the next morning saying, "You better get up. You're gonna be late for school."

– Chapter Seven –

Fishers of Men

It was January of 1972. Christmas had passed and the New Year had begun. On a Sunday, while driving home after church, I thought that if God was there, I must have missed Him. When I got home, I laid down on the green sectional sofa in the den feeling depressed and tired. The cat was warming herself on the sunlit window sill, and I, too, needed the warmth to provide some comfort from the aching I felt inside. As I was drifting off to sleep, the doorbell rang. Others were home. I rolled over, ignoring it. When it rang for the second time, I roused myself to answer the door, assuming it was a delivery for my dad, who ordered something from the pharmacy every day.

On the front porch stood three girls I had never seen before. They seemed similar in age, like juniors or seniors in high school. These girls had no idea who lived in the house, so they weren't seeking me out personally.

"Can I help you?" I asked.

One girl spoke as if they had already rehearsed and planned who would speak first. "We want to know if you believe in Jesus."

Rather than putting me off, it seemed to awaken my attention. I answered, "Yes."

"Have you been baptized in the Holy Spirit?" another asked.

"I was baptized when I was a few weeks old."

"We don't mean that. Can we come in to talk with you?"

We sat in my living room for a few minutes, having a conversation that seemed a bit awkward and somewhat disjointed. Jesus told his followers, "I will make you fishers of men," but these followers didn't seem to know what to do once they caught one.

Finally, one of them asked, "Will you drive down to the beach with us to talk with someone?"

We loaded into their VW bug and drove the thirty-minute drive to Jax Beach. I learned that they had first gone to the house next door and were told by Mrs. Stanley, my neighbor, that she wasn't interested. When they returned to their car one of them said, "Where to next?" They pulled the car up about a hundred feet to the next house—mine.

We arrived at a two-story, wood-sided house where some hippie-looking surfers, perhaps former drug addicts, now Christians, were living. We were invited into the living room, where we were met by a guy with long, sun-bleached hair who looked like a modern-day blonde-haired Jesus.

He shared for a while about the need we all have for a savior, and soon asked, "Do you want to pray for Jesus to come into your life and be filled with the Holy Spirit?"

We knelt on the round braided rug in the middle of the living room and I was led in a prayer traditionally known as the *Sinner's Prayer*. Without question, I was a sinner. After the prayer, all of them laid their hands on my head and asked God to fill me with the Holy Spirit. They began to pray with an utterance I had never heard before. The guy looked at me and said, "You can do this, too." I began to pray in a foreign-sounding tongue for about five seconds. Soon, like the Apostle Peter did when he stepped off the boat onto the water, I thought, "What am I doing?" I excused myself so I could go outside to smoke a cigarette.

Smoking a cigarette felt familiar to me, more so than what had just happened in the living room. After all, how often do you kneel with people you don't know in a living room, confess that you're a sinner, and speak in what sounds like gibberish that you've never heard before?

Still, I had a strong sense that three things had happened when I prayed. The first was that Something—whatever that Something was—had happened. The second was that my life as I had formerly known it would never be the same. It was as if my deepest yearning to start life all over again was coming true. Lastly, I had a sense that I had narrowly missed hell. The drive back to my home was quiet. When I got there, I went straight to my room, like so many other nights when I had come home wasted. This time, as I lay in bed, unable to sleep, I wondered: would this finally be the change I had longed for?

– Chapter Eight –
A Family Conference

As I drove to school the next morning, I turned off the radio to pray. It felt different to pull into the school parking lot sober. My aloneness didn't feel so alone.

I took classes both my junior and senior year with a woman who taught the Bible as history. Her salary was not paid by the public school system, so she had to raise her own support, like a missionary serving overseas. After homeroom, where attendance was taken, I quickly made my way to her classroom and announced across the room, "I found Jesus." She looked at me with a big smile. Everyone else in the classroom also heard what I said. By second period, others were asking me to tell them what had happened to me. During my study hall period, I sat with a group of people describing my experience at the beach house the evening before. I naively thought they would understand, but when I ended the story by saying that I'd given my life to God, everyone laughed. If they'd ever questioned my sanity, I had just confirmed to them all that I was truly nuts!

That evening, during dinner, I informed my parents that I wanted to have a family conference. My sister was away at college in Durham at my dad's alma mater, Duke

University, and my younger brother declined to come, preferring to watch the next episode of *Lost in Space*. Perhaps my parents told him it was okay not to come since they didn't know what in the world this family conference thing would be about. We'd never had a family conference. The three of us sat at the large cherrywood dining room table, where we ate only on special occasions. I burst into uncontrollable tears, overwhelmed by the idea that I had narrowly escaped death. If my life had continued the way it was going, I was becoming more and more convinced that I didn't want to keep living.

"I want to apologize for being a rotten son," I said. "I realize that if I had gotten busted for drugs, Dad's name would have appeared on the front page of the newspaper with 'junior' added to it." I wiped away my tears, trying to regain composure. "I want you to know that you don't need to worry about me any longer. I have given my life to God."

I don't think I'd ever seen such a worried look on their faces. My dad confessed that there was a time in his life he had thought about becoming a priest, something I'd never known. My mother shared that she and her childhood girlfriends would attend tent revival meetings, where they'd get emotional and go forward for the altar call. I believe the basic message they were attempting to communicate to me was: this too will pass.

But it didn't pass.

If there was one thing I had learned from my grand-mother's example of life, it was that being a Christian is more than just words. It's something you live. I knew I would need to live out my newfound faith, especially in my home with the people who knew me best.

I started to clean my room and do household chores without having to be asked. We had a maid who came every day to clean the house. One day, when she didn't show up, I cleaned the house, did the dishes, and made the beds.

When my mother came home from playing golf and bridge with her friends, she asked, "Has Dorothy already gone?"

I said, "She never came."

"Who cleaned the house?"

"I did."

When the same thing happened about a month later, I overheard my mother call my dad at his law office and in a whisper say, "He did it again." It was as if they wondered who had kidnapped their spoiled-rotten son and replaced him with someone responsible.

Not long after my experience at the beach house, I attended a party where everyone was getting high except for me. I likely had my Bible with me, as I was fascinated by the stories in it. Soon, no one asked me to go to these hangouts anymore, and truthfully, I didn't want to. I graduated from high school that year by the skin of my teeth, having to take two English credits during the last semester. Yet, for the first time, I made the honor roll.

That summer, I was outside mowing the yard when my girlfriend, Tillie Mendez-Vigo, drove from the beach to get me. Tilly was not only drop-dead gorgeous, but she was also a year older than me. She must have liked me because she bought a blue Camaro to match my rust-colored one. I was cool just by dating her.

Tillie could hardly contain herself when she pulled up, saying, "Get in. I met a group of people on the beach who are just like you. You have to meet them." I put away the mower and off we went.

When we got to the beach, the group was still there. I'd seen a recent issue of *TIME* magazine with the cover entitled *The Jesus Revolution,* and the group looked just like the pictures in the article. Tillie and I talked with a guy named Richard. He shared a story that would impact me for the rest of my life.

"When someone becomes a Christian," he said, "it is as if God pours a fresh drink of cool water inside to be shared with others, and who on this hot beach wouldn't like a drink of cool water? And when you give away the cool drink to someone, God refills the depleted supply in you to share with another."

I was sure the fresh cool drink of water God had poured into me was becoming tepid by now. My few experiences of telling others about my faith hadn't been well received, so I had adopted the view of just trying to live out the gospel in my life for others to see. Richard's words seemed to awaken in me what I sensed would become my life's vocation. I had no idea how, but it was clear to me what I wanted to do for the rest of my life, or at least try, which was to share with others the cool drink of water God had given me. I can't say my desire was utterly unselfish because I longed to be constantly re-freshed by God with the new cool water.

My life began to straighten up after coming to Christ. All the partying came to an end, my grades picked up, and my dad offered to buy me a new car. This would be my third car in three years. My first one had been a two-year-old olive green convertible GTO. One rainy evening, while out drinking a few beers with some friends, I had failed to notice the stopped traffic at a railroad crossing and ran into the back of someone. I was sixteen at the time. Fortunately, no one was hurt, but the GTO was totaled. My Dad was the attorney for a Chevrolet car dealer, so he took me to the lot and pointed out two Malibus and two Camaros.

"These are your choices," he said. None of them had as big of a motor as the GTO and none were convertibles, but I liked the bronze metallic color of the Camaro, so I settled on that one.

The Camaro I was still driving was barely a year old, but who wouldn't want a new car? My dad and I went down to a Plymouth dealership where I picked out the car of my dreams. At that moment, it was a Satellite Sebring Plus, gold with a cream-colored top and a larger engine. We ordered the car and would have to wait six weeks for it to arrive.

Before the new car came, I was attending a weekend youth retreat. During a plenary session, I suddenly became overwhelmed and went to my cabin to be alone. I fell on my knees and said prayers of surrender over everything I could think of. I surrendered my life anew to God, my wife if I should ever marry, my school, which I would gladly give up, and everything else that came to mind.

At one point I said, "I give you the new car that is coming soon." When I mentioned the new car, the oppressive feelings lifted.

I said aloud to God, "You want a new car?" I immediately prayed that God would work it out so that I wouldn't get it.

The following week I was passing my dad in the hallway on my way to school and he said, "You still want that new car, don't you?"

I said, "You know what? I don't. I'm quite satisfied with the one I have."

He said, "Great! I'll call and cancel it today."

Later that night I found out the car had arrived that day at the dealership. My dad told the salesman he no longer wanted it and to put the car on the lot to sell. The salesman was disappointed and ended up having words with my dad about how to raise kids. The car went on the lot because I'm sure the guy knew the legal fees he would incur trying to take my dad to court.

I would soon discover why it was important I didn't get a new car. There was, however, a bigger miracle taking place in the midst of all this. I, Neil Christopher Taylor, Jr., was, for once, actually satisfied and grateful for something I already had. Thanks be to God!

– Chapter Nine –
Nothing to Give

Who knew you were supposed to pray in a closet? In my youthful zeal to follow Jesus, I'd lock the door to my room, push my shoes aside, and kneel in my closet to pray. The night after Tillie and I met Richard on the beach, I prayed as I always did that my family would come to know Christ. When I finished praying, I had a sense that God said, "I have answered your prayers." I wondered how that could be since no one had come home saying they wanted to have a family conference to announce they had given their life to God. What I sensed next was something I'm not sure I wanted to hear, "I am giving you a Christian family."

My immediate response to God was, "If You're meaning the group of people I met today on the beach, You'll have to make it far more clear to me than just this one conversation."

Throughout the remainder of the summer, I attended Bible studies in the house where the group was living in downtown Jacksonville. Meanwhile, I made plans with a friend to attend a junior college in West Palm Beach. Tim and I had become friends during my last semester in high school. We had similar plans to get all our prerequisites done and then transfer to the University of Florida for our junior and senior years. Tim grew up a Baptist, and unlike myself, had always been a good kid. In late August, we moved into a garage apartment in West Palm Beach. The rent was a hundred dollars a month. Tim loved surfing, so moving close to a beach was a non-negotiable for him. I was never good at surfing, but I, too, loved the ocean, so when Tim went surfing, I'd often go share my faith with others at the beach, hoping to give away my cool drink of water before it could become tepid. Once, I ran into a foreigner, so I tried speaking in the foreign prayer language the way I and the others had in the beach house that day. The person looked more confused than when I was speaking English. Obviously, the foreign babble wasn't her native tongue.

I registered for the classes I was required to take and added whatever theology classes were offered. As I listened to an aged professor, I discovered I disagreed with almost everything he had to say. In his opinion, once the Holy Spirit came and helped start the early church, the Spirit left. But I knew without a doubt my life had been radically changed the evening I prayed and received the Holy Spirit. I can't say that a tongue of fire was on top of my head like on the day of Pentecost, but I did find the strength to finally put aside my former ways of living and began to live soberly. I didn't openly challenge the professor in class, but I knew I didn't want to listen to his teaching for a whole semester either. In some way, I'm sure this strengthened my desire to live together with others to grow in my relationship with God.

Every night after dinner I discussed with Tim whether I should move into the community with the group of people I'd met earlier that summer. Before I left to move to West Palm Beach, one of the members of the group had casually mentioned that he wished I was coming with them. It touched me deeply that someone actually wanted me with them. As much as I believed that God loved everyone, I'd never seen myself as someone lovable.

Tim said, during one of our after-dinner discussions, "Look, just don't try and talk me into going with you."

I replied, "No worries! I can hardly convince myself, let alone talk someone else into going, too."

It was the evening before the deadline to turn in textbooks for a full refund when a thought occurred to me: I lived in regret for many of the decisions I'd made apart from knowing Christ, and now there was a possibility I might live the same way, in regret, for not following Christ in the way I sensed Him leading me. What was there to lose? I returned my books the following morning for a full refund, packed all my belongings in my car, left a note for Tim with $50 for my part of the next month's rent, and began the six-hour trek on I-95 back to Jacksonville.

On the drive home, a Bible verse came to mind: *"But the natural man receiveth not the things of the Spirit of God: for they are foolishness unto him . . ."* (1 Cor. 2:14). In other words, I was quite certain that there was nothing I could say that was going to convince my parents, or anyone for that matter, that leaving everything to join an unknown community was a good idea.

I arrived home in Jacksonville around 11 p.m. My parents were in the midst of a bridge party with about a dozen of their friends. They were surprised to find me standing at the door.

My mother asked, "Why are you home so soon?" But she turned back to her guest and didn't hear my answer.

Only my dad heard me say, "I've dropped out of college and I'm going to join the group I met this summer."

My dad looked me straight in the eyes and said, "You need to know that you are throwing your life away." Interestingly, he practically quoted a scripture I'd been meditating on: *"Whoever seeks to save his life will lose it, and whoever loses his life will save it"* (Luke 17:33).

After the party ended that night, my mother, now aware of why I was home, woke me up at 2:00 a.m. and said, "You have nothing to give to anyone."

Surprisingly, I had my wits about me and responded, "You're right. I will have to learn."

When I awoke the next morning I discovered the Episcopal priest waiting for me in the living room. His advice sounded far more rational than mine as he encouraged me to finish school and then go to seminary afterward to become a priest. I laughed, saying, "I don't want to be a priest."

Not long after Father Gray left, my grandmother called to invite me out for lunch. My parents were pulling out all the "big guns" to talk me out of my plans. Mamma and I ate at the Lakewood pharmacy where we had eaten many meals together over the years. She offered me a job and said, "Then you'll have time to see after a few months if you still want to join the group."

No one understood more than I did the struggle it had been to make this decision. I told her, "I'm afraid if I wait, I won't go."

When I drove out of the parking lot, I saw my grandmother wiping tears from her eyes in my rearview mirror. It broke my heart to disappoint her.

Twenty years later, while attending a seminary course

in the 90s, I heard a professor say, "If you can talk yourself out of a calling, by all means, do."

I tried in every way possible at the time, but at every turn, I became more and more convinced about what I believed God was calling me to do. When I moved into the community that September of 1972, it had only been nine months from the prayer experience late that Sunday afternoon in the beach house when I sensed God the Holy Spirit said to me, "Life as you have known it will never be the same."

I could never have imagined how true that would be.

– Chapter Ten –
Leaving Home

That Saturday afternoon in September of 1972, I hugged my parents goodbye, not knowing when I would see them again. We stood in the same spot on the front steps where I had stood nine months earlier with those three girls who asked if I wanted to surrender my life to Jesus. I was eighteen years old and my encounter with them had set in motion a relationship that would profoundly affect the rest of my life. Not only mine but my parents as well. Fighting back tears, I drove away from the only home I had ever known.

The group of Jesus People had moved from Jacksonville to Gainesville, and I didn't have an address. On the drive to Gainesville, I found myself pondering the verse from the gospels, *"If anyone comes to me and does not hate father and mother, wife and children, brothers and sisters —yes, even their own life—such a person cannot be my disciple"* (Luke 14:26). I knew I didn't hate my parents or siblings, even though that was probably their perception based on the choices I was making. All I knew was that I sincerely wanted to follow Jesus in whatever way that meant.

By the time I got to Gainesville, it was nearly dinner

time, so I pulled into a Steak and Shake restaurant. When the waitress brought the food to my car, I asked, "Have you seen a big red school bus with four-foot-tall letters on the side spelling JESUS?"

"Try heading west on Main Street," she said. "I think I saw that bus down there." It was rather conspicuous.

Within five minutes I spotted it in front of a green, wooden, two-story house with a big front porch in much need of a paint job. No one had any idea I was coming, so there wasn't a welcoming party of any sort. I had never even asked anyone if I could come. It was 1972, so there wasn't such a thing as an online application to fill out. With the community being all of about four months old, organizational standards were yet to be developed.

The group of about twenty-five people had only been living in the rented house for a couple of weeks when I got there, so the furnishings were sparse. Someone had made the effort to make things feel like home by hanging pictures on the walls and arranging whatever furniture had been gathered. The house was quiet when I arrived since some people had gone to a local prayer meeting in town. Communal living typically raises suspicions, so it was always intentional for the community to establish relationships with other Christians in the area. There were five or six bedrooms upstairs that were given to the married couples and one designated to the single women. The men rolled out sleeping bags in the living room each night. Someone pointed out where I'd be sleeping, so I laid out my sleeping bag with my opened suitcase serving as my dresser drawer.

The day had felt like an eternity, beginning with my early morning meeting with the priest. After that, I had lunch with my grandmother, which was heartbreaking for us both. I had found my way to this house by hunting for a big red bus in a city I'd never been to. Now I was sitting in a somewhat empty house believing I was following God and my heart's desire. I was both exhausted and relieved after months of contemplating this decision and trying to imagine the outcome of actually doing it. Tim was probably content to have the garage apartment all to himself and no longer have to engage with me over my inner convictions. I wouldn't see Tim again for thirty-six years until we met for dinner at a Cracker Barrel in Jacksonville where we would talk about our relationship with God with as much ease as if we'd just spoken the evening before. My longing was to simply know where God wanted me to be, and after that, I figured I'd discover what he wanted me to do. Walking through the door of that house in Gainesville felt like I had arrived home.

Then a dreaded reality hit me. I had left my two pillows on my bed at my parents' house in Jacksonville. I'm a side sleeper, perhaps due to the long scar that wraps around my torso, and I like having an extra pillow. I had remembered to bring pillowcases, so I stuffed one with some clothes and folded up my jacket to use as my head pillow. Whatever peace I felt about having finally arrived was replaced with irritation for being so absent-minded.

I was stretched out on my sleeping bag when the front door swung open. The group was arriving home from the prayer meeting they'd attended. A guy named John announced, "We got a donation of bedding. Anybody need a pillow?" A pillow flew across the room and hit me in the face; I perceived it as a gift from God. As I lay down in the hallway on my sleeping bag that night in a place I'd never been with people I didn't know, I sensed God say to me, *"The Son of Man had nowhere to lay his head, but I've given you a pillow. Welcome home, son."*

—

There were many things about communal living I wasn't prepared for, and one had immediate consequences. The dietary changes caused me to have diarrhea for the first three days. Most of the meals were heavy on starch, and the USDA recommended dietary requirements of four to six ounces of meat per meal was a thing of the past. We often received leftover food from local business meetings and church potlucks. A typical evening snack consisted of canned K-rationed bread from the Vietnam war with some peanut butter spread on top. It was quite a change from the leftovers at my mom's, where she always had my favorite waffle mix available in the refrigerator. When I discovered it was the Winn Dixie grocery stores that donated the meat used in their advertising photo shoots, I didn't bother telling anybody that the founder of Winn Dixie was my step-grandfather. His private jet had flown me home after my surgery in North Carolina when I was twelve years old.

The daily routine in the community involved doing chores after breakfast, followed by what we called a "body meeting." It was simply a carry-over term from the "student body meetings" in high school. Eventually, we changed the name to "community gatherings" because of some of the unfortunate connotations of the phrase "body meeting." Each morning, we met to listen to a Bible-teaching tape by popular Christian teachers such as

Charles Stanley, Bob Mumford, Corrie Ten Boom, or Chuck Swindoll, and afterward spent time in worship singing songs, sharing prayer requests, and listening to daily announcements. After lunch, the majority of us would head out to witness to others about our newfound relationship with Jesus. We spent a lot of time around the University of Florida campus and now and then I'd run into high school acquaintances. Those chance meetings felt a bit awkward now that I was growing a beard and mustache and my hair was getting long, making me look more hippy-like and less preppy. I'm sure those who saw me wondered, "What in the world happened to that guy?"

The average age of most of the community members was twenty. The leaders, a married couple named Dawn and John Herrin, were the exception. They were twenty years older than the rest of us. Dawn was thin and attractive, though she wouldn't have thought so. She wore steel-rimmed glasses and kept her hair pulled back. Her husband John looked like an older hippy. He was somewhat withdrawn, with glasses and a thick mustache and goatee. He could command everyone's attention with his sermons but was not approachable on a personal level. He seemed to attract or offend women with nothing in between. I'd later discover that Dawn's practical, down-to-earth wisdom was partially due to her husband's periodic alcoholism. Their children, Wendi, John, and Katherine, were all part of the community. Wendi was married to Glenn Kaiser and John married his fifteen-year-old high school sweetheart, Tina, in Alabama, with a permission slip from her mother. They had joined the fledgling community of Jesus People in Milwaukee, Wisconsin, in the height of the Jesus Movement that took place in the late 60s and early 70s. Dawn always said she felt like she had died and gone to heaven by being a part of a community of young people who loved and desired to follow Jesus. The atmosphere of enthusiasm differed from the infidelity and instability of life with her husband, John. Dawn was someone I would describe as having both feet on the ground, which isn't a description I would have used for myself. In many ways, she was the heart and soul of the community and gave everything she had to fan the flame of zeal that existed in those early days of the Jesus Movement. In the same way that Jesus trusted those twelve young disciples to carry forth his message, Dawn believed in us. What I couldn't know then was that Dawn would, in many ways, become my mother, my pastor, my colleague, and friend, and remain an important part of my life for the next forty years.

Before I left Jacksonville for good I had had the forethought to ask my father who officially owned my flashy sports car. I hadn't paid for it. He said it was mine and signed over the title. I gave the keys to the community, and it was sold two weeks later to help pay bills. With nowhere to go and no money to spend, I certainly did not need the car. We lived hand to mouth, something that had never been part of my childhood.

When my parents came to visit me a month later, I think they were hoping I would be tired of the communal experiment. They had no idea of the stress I had gone through before finally deciding to leave everything to follow Jesus. I knew what I wanted to do with my life, and had some idea about how I wanted to attain those goals by living together with others who had similar desires.

One incident that stood out as a reminder of how

limited I had felt in my parents' suburban home happened on a hot sweltering day when I invited the two black men who were mowing our yard to come inside for something cold to drink. I knew these men from when I was a kid because they worked for my grandmother at the cemetery. When my mother came home, she discovered us sitting around the kitchen table talking and enjoying some ice tea. No words were exchanged, but the men hastily returned to their work, sensing my mother's disapproval of them being in the house. It was never discussed, like most things in our home, but I was painfully aware of the racist attitude that dominated the South. One evening, I had to leave the dining room when the discussion became about black people's brains being smaller than white people's. In my opinion, whoever believed that had just shown whose brain was smaller.

During their visit to Gainesville, my parents took me for lunch at a nice restaurant and tried to talk me into coming back home. I don't think my mother ate much of the shrimp cocktail she ordered. My absence was more painful to them than I could realize. I discovered some years later that my mother told Dawn, "In some ways, Neil being in this community seems worse than death. What do we say to our friends at the country club and other social gatherings when they talk about their children attending this or that university?" My parents certainly weren't going to brag about me joining a commune. Charles Manson's community was not that far out of people's minds. I was glad they came to see me, but I doubt they felt the same. I imagine my mother probably cried all the way back home. The last thing I wanted to do was upset my parents, but, no doubt, I had.

– Chapter Eleven –
A Heart of Flesh

While some people made rhymes with my name, others conjured up nicknames for me. One of the sisters (we called each other brother and sister in the community) referred to me as the 'holy of holies' because I was so eerily quiet. I don't think I realized how withdrawn and introspective I had become. I had spent so much time hiding the real Neil from others, I, too, had lost track of him. Hiding from others started before I ever knew that was what I was doing. In first grade, I once opened my lunch box and discovered a small thermos with warm spaghetti inside. I quickly screwed the lid back on, not wanting others to know I had something special that they didn't have. As I got older, my desperate need to hide from others caused me to end up losing myself. I now desired to be transparent but had little experience doing so. I felt I had nothing to lose and maybe everything to gain.

My deeply held fear was that if people got to know me, they wouldn't like me. From my point of view, there wasn't much to like. Life had always been focused on whatever made me happy with little concern for others and what their needs were. Living a double life brought about awkward twists and unspoken lies between me and others. My opinion was that others were better off steering clear of me, and many were smart enough to do so. Even though I was now a new person in Christ, I was more familiar with the person I used to be, the Neil I knew most and didn't like. In time, I hoped to become a new Neil and build a friendship with my new self. My hope was that I would become someone I liked, and I became willing to take the risk that others might like me too.

Conversely, as a young, enthusiastic, inexperienced eighteen-year-old Christian, I naively believed I loved everyone. After living with others in community for only a couple of months, I realized the opposite was the truth. I didn't love anyone.

While in prayer, I sensed God nudging me to become transparent with others. I'd lived in the community for six months and rarely spoke to anyone without it being a response to a question. I was raised in the South, so outwardly I had good manners and was polite. One of my mentors, Jean Vanier, said, "We can be polite and not loving." I was that—polite and not loving.

One morning, when we were gathered for our time of worship and prayer, the person leading asked if anyone had anything they wished to share. I hesitantly raised my hand and said, "Maybe some people see me as spiritual because I am so quiet. It's not about being spiritual. It's about being afraid. I fear if I allow others to know me then they won't like me, so I don't take the risk. I believe God has shown me that this stems from being selfish. Yes, I am afraid to let others know me, but I am also selfish by being unwilling to take the time to get to know others, and for that, I apologize. I want to change, and I want to be your friend."

Afterward, one person approached me and said, "I will be your friend." It may not seem like a great success, but to go from no friends to one friend in only a few minutes was a huge gain. Janet Cameron is still my friend today.

The Bible says, "*I will give you a new heart and put a new spirit in you; I will remove from you your heart of stone and give you a heart of flesh*" (Ezekiel 36:26). I had to face the truth that, even if my heart was transforming from a heart of stone to a heart of flesh, it was still only about the size of a BB. I would now have to live out my words by being interested in others and not only myself.

Nearly fifty years later, I like to think that my heart of flesh now measures near the size of a golf ball. Since a normal heart is the size of an orange, I still have a long way to go. At sixty-seven, I've resolved I won't make it in this lifetime to be fully changed into the new creation all are promised to become in Christ. But I am eternally grateful for the changes that have transpired thus far.

—

My quietness in the group was partly due to another thing about myself that I hid from others: I was very near-sighted and had thrown my glasses away. I wasn't able to see people's expressions very clearly. If someone smiled at me, I couldn't see it. There was a prosperity teaching at the time referred to as "name it and claim it." The belief was that if your faith was strong enough, you could claim healing for whatever and then you simply had to follow through with it as if it were a fact. I would later learn that this false teaching is an attempt to control God, trying to make Him do whatever you want. I was determined and deceived to demonstrate faith by my actions, which in my immaturity meant to throw away my glasses. I hate to think about the people I put at risk. I had driven from Jacksonville to Gainesville on unfamiliar roads without glasses. Fortunately, finding a big red bus wasn't so difficult.

Part of the daily routine in the community was to go out in groups of two or three every afternoon to share our faith with others. One day, I was sent out with two sisters, Judy and Jeanne. At the end of our day, while we were waiting for the bus to pick us up, Judy mentioned that she needed prayer because the devil was lying to her saying she couldn't see. Before we could pray, Jeanne confessed the devil was lying to her, too, saying that she couldn't see either. Of course, there I stood as blind as a bat, so I said, "Well, the devil sure is doing a lot of lying today, because he's telling me I can't see either." Scripture does say that *"the devil is the father of all lies"* (John 8:44). But sometimes he doesn't need to lie, because we do it for him. When the bus arrived, the three of us managed to find an empty seat, none the wiser or seeing any clearer.

Nearly a year later, my friend and mentor Dawn and I ended up having a moment by ourselves. She casually said, "You know, I believe God could heal a person from nearsightedness with their glasses on as well as with them off. While wearing your glasses, you would suddenly be unable to see until you removed them." I later discovered that when my parents had visited me in Gainesville, a month after I moved into the community, my mother told Dawn I'd stopped wearing my glasses.

I called my mother that night and asked her to send me a pair of glasses. As I look back on that year of near blindness, there was a miracle that took place, but not with my eyes being restored to perfect vision. Rather it had to do with me growing in the ability to recognize wisdom and good sense. I can't help but wonder if my mother noticed, too.

– Chapter Twelve –
A New Life

Late in 1972, I called home to tell my parents I would not be home for Christmas. The Jesus People community was traveling north, where the majority of the members lived. I'd never spent Christmas apart from my family and they were unhappy about my decision. After the New Year, we spent four months traveling the Upper Peninsula of Michigan in a school bus visiting small towns to hold what we called Jesus rallies. They were similar to tent revival meetings, but certainly not held in a tent in the Upper Peninsula during the winter.

I didn't even know there was another peninsula besides Florida, but one thing I quickly learned was that the climate there was nothing like the peninsula where I grew up. I wore every bit of clothing I had in that bitter cold. When I received a gift of twenty-five dollars from my grandmother for my birthday, I immediately bought a pair of long underwear, the quilted type. At times I could be seen wearing them over my regular clothes.

These "Jesus Rallies" were held in school auditoriums and civic centers. They consisted of Christian rock-n-roll interspersed with a couple of skits from our drama group, the Holy Ghost Players. The rallies always concluded with a gospel message and an altar call for those who wanted to commit their lives to Christ. It wasn't uncommon to see two hundred or more people make commitments to Christ in these small towns of five thousand or less. We were experiencing our version of a Billy Graham-type crusade in what seemed to me like a foreign country—the U.P. I had often prayed to God saying I would go anywhere in the world, and the U.P. felt like Siberia.

Our community never returned to Florida. Instead, I had begun a journey that would land me in Chicago, Illinois, where I would make my home for the next forty-four years.

Life on the road in a school bus in the dead of winter in Michigan made us all long for a place of our own. The turnout for the Jesus rallies was invigorating enough to keep us going, but Dawn, who had the uncommon re-source of good sense, knew we couldn't keep up the pace much longer. In April 1973, she, along with a carload of others, including me, headed to Chicago to scout out possibilities of a place for us to call home.

We were invited to stay in the basement of a worship facility called Faith Tabernacle on the corner of Broadway and Grace Streets. How apropos! The area was called New Town and included the famous Wrigley Field, the Chicago Cubs stadium.

Faith Tabernacle had once been the Marigold Wrestling Arena. It was purchased by a Christian man in the late 60s to use during a revival called Christian Growth Ministries. At one time it was a booming church with over a thousand people attending, but when we arrived in May 1973, all that remained of the congregation were a couple dozen needy senior citizens. The organization had packed up and moved the headquarters to Florida. We immediately began caring for these seniors by shopping for them, transporting them to doctor's appointments, and assisting them with their household duties. One older lady named Halley had nine cats in her apartment. The smell was enough to send a non-allergic person into anaphylactic shock.

The church was in a kind of "has been" state, to put it mildly. The two pastors were a husband and wife team who positioned themselves as faith healers. I witnessed some bizarre services, such as the time the woman pastor proclaimed she knew God was renewing her healing ministry in a mighty way because her finger was turning green. She held it up for her husband to inspect as he leaned in for a closer look and attested to its green hue. Perhaps she had slammed it in a drawer the previous day. The few elderly who were left behind seemed to all marvel at this supposedly new movement of God in their midst.

Once, a close friend of mine, Glenn Kaiser, had a terrible earache and decided to go forward to receive prayer for healing. The male pastor proceeded to stick his finger rather forcefully into Glenn's ear as he excitedly pronounced, "Be healed." Glenn screamed and nearly passed out from the pain, which was both terrible and hilarious at the same time. Evidently, the male pastor did not have a green finger like his wife.

Our stay at the church was supposed to be temporary as we looked for a house to rent. As time went on, I found myself talking to a girl who had moved into our community from St. Joseph, Michigan, just before we started traveling through the U.P. Pegge was a student at the local college, and after some conversation with a few of the members, she packed a bag and told her parents she was leaving with us. There was a rule in the community that men and women were not supposed to spend too much one-on-one time together, but that rule was continually stretched to its limits. I liked Pegge because she was pretty and laughed at my jokes. We talked so often that her mentor in the community had to reprimand her for flirting too much with me.

Pegge and I weren't the only ones neglecting the rules. Several couples married within the first two years of the community being together. We accommodated newlyweds by building 8'x8' rooms in the church basement out of two-by-fours and cheap paneling. I'm not sure how it got started, but we called the little rooms "barcelonas." One couple managed to put a waterbed in their "barcelona" that practically took up the whole room. Visiting with them meant you risked becoming seasick since the waterbed was the only place to sit.

One day I asked to speak to the leader of the community and sought permission to ask Pegge to marry me. That's how it was done at that time. It was a way of being respectful and seeking guidance. Basically, you were asking, "Do you think I am mature enough for this?" Or, "Do you have anything you want to say to me about this decision?"

Not long after, while walking through Lincoln Park Zoo in Chicago, I managed to be alone with Pegge and asked her to marry me.

"Are you crazy?" she said.

"Yes."

She said she'd think about it.

"OK," I said. "I'll ask you again in a couple of days."

She laughed. A few days later when I asked again, to

my surprise, she said yes. We were engaged for three months.

Much of my life as a Christian has been about feeling "led." I haven't always been right about what I have felt led to do, but a sense of intuition has played a significant role in fueling my motivation. Getting married was something I did because I felt led. Even though we traveled on a bus together for four months, I can honestly say that I hardly knew Pegge. The truth was that despite being with the same people morning, noon, and night, I didn't know how to have a deep relationship with anyone. It was one more thing I would have to learn.

Pegge and I were married in 1974 in her hometown of St. Joseph, which is about a hundred miles from Chicago on the other side of Lake Michigan. It was the coldest day of the year. Despite bad weather, my family was able to fly in to be present for the wedding. Everyone from the community traveled on the bus that Saturday morning to attend. My mother-in-law insisted on having the reception at Win Shuler's, a popular upscale restaurant known throughout Michigan for their cheese spread. Pegge's mother, Alice, was obvious in her disdain for the leader of our community, John Herrin, Sr. After the wedding, Alice informed him that none of the community members were invited to the reception. Alice didn't realize that my grandmother was on the other side of the coat rack, hidden from view, and overheard the conversation. Mamma found John afterward and said, "Please have everyone come and I'll pay for all the Jesus People to have a meal if there's not enough food. Neil and Pegge would be severely disappointed if all of you weren't there."

When Mamma got into my parents' car to drive over

to the restaurant, she asked my parents if either of them had brought a checkbook. They hadn't and wanted to know why she was asking. When they heard what Mamma had offered, my mother scolded her for her breach of etiquette.

"It's too late now," Mamma said. This was another gift my grandmother had—she could purposefully make something unfixable when necessary. I learned about this exchange a year after we were married. Mamma saved the reception, unbeknownst to anyone except my parents. If members of the community had been sent home, I'm quite sure Pegge and I would have left Win Shuler's to have our reception back in Chicago. Instead, I have a wonderful picture of my grandmother sitting at a table with many of the Jesus People, laughing and carrying on. It's just one more memory of an exceptional dining event with my grandmother.

For our honeymoon, my family gave us a trip to Israel. After spending four days in Mystic, Connecticut, we joined a Christian tour group to fly to Israel. Part of the experience included attending a convention with the acclaimed faith healer Kathryn Kuhlman. I still secretly hoped that my vision would be restored and that was part of my desire to honeymoon there. My vision was not healed, but my eyes were opened in other ways.

In retrospect, I wouldn't recommend that young newlyweds join a tour group as part of their honeymoon. Being on a tight schedule immediately highlighted some of the differences between Pegge and me. I'm a morning person; Pegge isn't. I like to be somewhere on time; Pegge likes to be fashionably late, which doesn't work well when there is a bus full of people waiting to leave for a sightseeing tour. She thinks in black and white, and I don't. I was still a teenager and somewhat of a social misfit, and now I had taken a vow to navigate life with a partner very different from myself. For us to make a decision about anything often felt like a negotiation. I did wonder while on our honeymoon if getting married had been a mistake.

Luckily, we had the advantage of living in a community with other couples, which helped provide perspective and adjust our expectations. I realized that I would not be diminished when I didn't get my way, which was a novel thing for me. Gradually, I became less picky, more patient, and learned the art of compromise. Marriage was like being transplanted into a hothouse to grow. The glue that held Pegge and me together was God's grace and our calling to live in community with others. I was fortunate to marry a person who never questioned our communal lifestyle and sense of call. During our first year of marriage, we lived in a Sunday School classroom because all the spaces in the basement were being used. We had to vacate our room every Sunday. We'd push our thin foam mattress against the wall, stuff our belongings into suitcases, and move out for the day. Life was meager, but it was good.

– Chapter Thirteen –
A Matter of Grace

Our temporary stay in the Faith Tabernacle basement stretched into two years, by which time the church was, understandably, eager for us to move out. Our community was growing. When a group is willing to take in the people others don't know what to do with, people find you. We welcomed a pregnant single woman with no place to go, a drug-addicted daughter of a doctor from the east coast, a fifteen-year-old boy who got his mother to sign a permission slip so he could move in with us, and an occasional street urchin, as some might call them, who had no place to call home.

We occupied every available room in the church facility, and there had to be at least six to eight "barcelonas" in the basement by now. We prayed daily to find a place of our own.

One morning, I realized our prayers had been answered. I had just turned twenty-one years old and had come of age to inherit money left to me by my mother's mother, Grandma Nonnie, in the form of stocks. I called my parents and asked them to sell my shares, which went over like a lead balloon.

"That is not what your grandmother left you the money for," my mother said.

"I wasn't aware that she attached any directives to her gift," I said.

My parents were using their inheritance from my grandmother to buy riverfront property near my childhood home.

"I want to do the same thing you're doing," I pointed out. "I want to buy a house. The only difference is that mine won't be just for me, but for the community."

Eventually, my dad got on the phone. "I can make it so you will never see that money," he told me.

"I'm sure you can, so if Nonnie meant for you to have the money she left me then go ahead, take it. But if the stock was left for me, then I'm asking that you please sell it and send the money to me, so we can purchase a house."

The call ended abruptly. A week later, my mother called and said, "The stock sold for fifteen thousand dollars and the check is in the mail to you." The exchange on the phone was actually pleasant.

Maybe they were finally beginning to accept that I was making my own decisions in life. It was around this time that my mother said to me, "It's not you I worry about. It's your brother and sister." How I got off her worry list was a mystery to me.

With the money, we were able to begin negotiations to purchase our first piece of real estate, a six-flat apartment building in the Ravenswood area of Chicago. Today that neighborhood is the home of former Chicago Mayor Rahm Emmanuel, but when we moved in, it had a fair amount of gang activity. The Jesus People community seemed to over-whelm most gangs, or at least stifle their activity. Our vibe was quite different. Someone jokingly referred to us as the Almighty Jesus People Nation. I'm sure we looked more similar to the Beverly Hillbillies when we arrived with our sparse belongings all packed into a big red school bus with the name 'Jesus' painted in four-foot-tall letters on the side. One of the tenants didn't vacate for a year, so roughly a hundred of us moved into the remaining five apart-ments. There were four married couples in each, and the front living rooms were turned into dorms with triple-bunk beds for either single men or single women. Roughly twenty people shared the two bathrooms in each apartment with a common area and kitchen on each floor serving as a space to have small meetings and celebrations. One side of the basement became our kitchen, and the other side served as our dining room and multi-purpose room.

It was crowded, so illnesses were hard to confine. One of the community members contracted hepatitis after eating raw oysters while on vacation. The sickness spread quickly and was easily identified by the yellowing of eyes and skin. A doctor friend prescribed gamma globulin shots for everyone in the community. The floor I lived on became the quarantine area for the single men who were infected.

This event helped define an area of pastoral care for me. I began to cook for all the men in quarantine. High protein was an essential part of the cure. With the little knowledge I had about nutrition, I began making scram-bled eggs, bacon, and toast for breakfast and, of course, grits, since I'm from the South, and hamburgers for lunch. Soon I was asked to give pastoral care to those working in the kitchen, which earned me the nickname "the pastor of disaster." Any careful reading of the Old Testament will affirm that the topic of food can be a volatile one and much grumbling can come from the way it's prepared. Kitchen meetings in our community were historically tense and required continual intervention and reconciliation. When suggestions to cut the food budget were brought up in leadership meetings, I would argue that it was like the federal government threatening to cut Medicare and Social Security as the cure to the economy. I would always propose some budget cuts elsewhere before we spent less on one of the few everyday pleasures like our meals. I had heard Dawn say many times, even when we were flat broke, there's always money for ice cream. After all, cooking for a few hundred people brings huge challenges on its own without trying to nickel and dime every aspect of food prep.

Participating in the kitchen and dish room was often a place of entry for a new person or visitor in the community. Some were from other countries with limited skills in English, which often gave way to some comedic events. One time a woman from Germany thought the head cook told her to put the plastic bin of ingredients in the oven. The smell of burning plastic quickly filled the kitchen. Another person took creative license by putting cloves in the pancake batter. The head cooks were invaluable to us, though oftentimes their skills for large-scale cooking had to be acquired mostly through trial and error, and everyone experienced their learning curve. Measurements were not made in cups but in gallons, and a can of something was a #10 size can. A pinch of something was typically a fistful and we all suffered from too much spice, too much garlic, too much salt, or not enough. All seminarians should oversee kitchens; it's a great place to learn pastoral care.

Like the cooks I oversaw in the kitchen, I was deve-loping my own recipe for spiritual success. I kept a strict discipline of reading and praying and began believing that these practices earned my right-standing with God. But, once again, God was about to step in and show me that I had much to learn.

Less than a year after my marriage to Pegge, I was admitted to Grant Hospital in Chicago with severe intes-tinal pain. I had not been hospitalized for my congenital condition of portal vein thrombosis since seventh grade. Of course, I called my staunchest advocate—my dad. He and my mother flew up immediately. The surgeon wanted to operate, but after listening to his reasons, my dad said no. I wasn't bleeding, and eventually, the blockage passed and I returned to the community. I had a clean bill of health as well as a hefty bill for $5,000 that I couldn't pay.

My dad took care of the hospital charges, but not with-out complaint. When my grandmother heard him grum-bling, she was aghast. She said she would sell her house in a heartbeat if it was a matter of maintaining my health.

I was reminded of that unshakable foundation I was so fortunate to have, that I was born into a world where others wanted and loved me. Yet I had come to believe that I was not lovable simply for being me. During my hospital stay, I couldn't keep up with my daily spiritual practices. As I lay there, all I did was watch TV. Reading and praying just put me to sleep, which in the end was probably what I needed most. Someone brought me a tape that I listened to on my cassette recorder entitled, *The Cross Cancels Satan's Claims*. One of the claims canceled by the death of Jesus was condemnation. I was confronted with the reality of God's love for me as unconditional and not dependent on my daily practices. Even while I felt lazy and complacent, the truth of Romans 5:8 struck home: *"But God showed his great love for us by sending Christ to die for us while we were still sinners."* That was me—still a sinner. And if he loved me while I was yet a sinner, He loved me during my convalescence, when I had no desire to read the Bible or pray. This matter of understanding the grace of God became the most essential ingredient and foundation for all of life ahead.

Two months after being released from the hospital I was asked to be on the leadership team for the community. I don't think I would have been qualified to offer pastoral support to any in our community, if I hadn't had this lesson of understanding life through the lens of God's unconditional love, Grace.

– Chapter Fourteen –
An Island of Misfits

The birth of a community is no small thing. My view is that the gestation period is twice as long as an elephant's, which is two years. Many people who decide to try communal living do not survive for long, a year or two at most. Jean Vanier said, "There is always enough energy for take-off." There are moments of splendor, but it can quickly grow tiresome. And crowded. We opened our lobby and dining room as a place for homeless people to sleep during freezing winter nights. Those who joined us for worship on a Sunday morning would see the mats all stacked and some of the homeless often stayed for church, especially since beans and rice were served afterward. One young man who was contemplating joining our community was told by his Moody Bible Institute professor, "Oh, don't do that. You might start to smell like them."

Someone described us as being like the Muppets. What a fantastic analogy! We were absolutely a living example of God's loving, diverse characters.

Early in our history, there was a couple who visited our group often from their hometown in Michigan. They would leave their children at home with the grandparents and spend long weekends with us in Chicago. They regularly treated others to deep-dish pizza and movies, so it was always great fun to see them. Eventually, they decided to take the plunge and move in. They sold their business and their home and turned over $25,000 to us, which we used right away to publish our magazine, *Cornerstone*. We always had to pay for the printing in advance.

One week later, the couple decided to leave. Their car was still theirs to drive away, but the money they had given was already spent. It was a dreadful lesson learned. Sadly, we never heard from them again. How much better for them and us if they had continued to just visit and enjoy movies and deep-dish pizza.

After that, we instituted a guideline that anyone interested in joining had to visit for a week or two so they could experience day-to-day life in the community. We also didn't allow new members to turn over assets until they had lived in the community for a year. The honeymoon phase ends differently for every person, but it does end.

A single mother found her way to us when she was pregnant with her fourth child. I was told all the children had different fathers, none of whom were still in the picture. She needed help with her children while she gained stability and prepared for the birth of her fourth child.

My wife Pegge and I were asked if we would care for two of the children, the youngest, a boy of eight, and the oldest, a twelve-year-old girl. The middle child was a ten-year-old boy who stayed with another couple for a year or two. Eventually, the middle child came under our care as well. Pegge was in early pregnancy with our first child, but we agreed to take responsibility for the children, believing it would be of service to the woman and help us prepare for family life ourselves. The children saw their mother every day and spent every Saturday with her, so it wasn't as if she disappeared from their lives.

Pegge and I tried our best to provide a family life for the children, taking them on vacations and on holidays to meet our families. Since my parents lived in Florida, we were able to take them to Sea World and Disney World.

Our daughter, Mindy, was born on Labor Day in 1978. My parents flew up to meet their first grandchild. It was hotter than blue blazes in Chicago that year and even native Floridians found the heat difficult. Of course, most things in Florida are air-conditioned. Our six-flat didn't have central air, only window fans. My parents wanted to buy us a window unit, but I told them not to. It would be another ten to fifteen years before AC units were commonly used, and even then, our building could barely support the electrical load. It wasn't uncommon during the hot summer nights for families to bring sleeping bags to the cooled common areas to sleep, so that's what we did.

Caring for the children was more of a challenge than we expected. We had no real knowledge of what the kids had been exposed to or what their experiences had been previously. We understood they had different fathers, but we never thought to ask what the home life had been like. We were too young and inexperienced to know what questions to ask. Eventually, we discovered that the youngest boy required extra supervision since he was often getting into trouble with other kids.

We continued to care for the children for a couple more years until the birth of our second daughter, Kirsten.

By this time, the woman had become a responsible member of the community and ended up marrying a stable, mature man in our community. Not long after, they decided to move out with all the children. Pegge and I were somewhat relieved to be free of the responsibility and were ready to focus on our own family. We considered this period of surrogate parenting as one chapter in our lives, and now we could move on to the next. Little did we realize that one of the children would one day reappear, delivering accusations that would lead to consequences I could not have imagined.

– Chapter Fifteen –

The Friendly Towers

As a community, we were accustomed to living in tight quarters. We had made our home in a church basement, then outfitted a six-unit building to house more than one hundred people. But after three years our membership was nearing two hundred and we were once again bursting at the seams. At one point, a mostly black community of about thirty people from the south side of Chicago decided to move in with us on the north side. We had met a few people from this community a couple of years earlier while witnessing on the streets in downtown Chicago. I would be blessed to serve in a co-pastor relationship with one of their elders, Ron Brown, for the next thirty years. Ron and I shared many of the same tasks, basically doing what felt like being on call in an emergency room, always available to the community members' everyday needs and crises. Ron was twelve years my senior, and his kindness and jovial spirituality were both a model and inspiration to me. Though neither of us holds the position we used to, we are still in touch to this day.

In 1978, the community sold the apartment building to buy a corridor building in the Uptown neighborhood of Chicago. We had been providing ministry in this notoriously impoverished area for some time, delivering large donations of food from local bakeries and grocers to the many needy families living there. When the Uptown Greater Food Depository came into existence, Jesus People were the first to volunteer. The four-story building we purchased was called the Friendly Towers and was classified as an SRO—single room occupancy. It was in a particularly rough area of Uptown. Not many business-men or developers were willing to take on such a property, but we saw it as an opportunity to stand in the gap where there was a need. Sometimes, effective ministry is accom-plished by those who aren't dominated by a fear of doing something wrong. Perhaps our shared life in community gave us the courage to move forward and take on feats that the average person wouldn't. None of us dared to venture out alone after dark. Gunshots were a normal part of the ambiance. One member was grazed by a bullet while standing in front of the Friendly Towers. Luckily, he wore thick glasses that shattered, which kept him from being hurt. Individually we could have never accomplished much of what we did, but together it seemed we'd muster enough wisdom and good sense to keep moving forward. Somehow things always worked out and daily provisions were provided.

As word of our ministries spread, more needy people came to the Friendly Towers looking for food. Our motto was that there was always an extra peanut butter and jelly sandwich for someone. Making sandwiches became part of the receptionist's job. We began to invite people in to share a meal with us during our regular meal times and eventually found there wasn't enough seating for our guests and the community members. One of the guests suggested we serve them earlier, before our meal. We did and began feeding an additional two hundred people per day. The food line in front of our home on Malden Street was not a welcome sight for some of our neighbors. We didn't know it at the time, but feeding and sheltering homeless people during the bitter winter would ultimately pave the way for the Jesus People community to become a recognized social service in the City of Chicago.

– Chapter Sixteen –
A Crusty Old Heart

My grandmother Mamma had few vices, but she enjoyed betting on horses. Every Thanksgiving she would visit her brother, my Great Uncle Neil, in New Orleans. She limited her gambling to fifty dollars. Once she won the daily double and gave me, my brother, and sister each a hundred and seventy-five dollars when she returned. I had gone with Mamma to New Orleans a few times when I was young but hadn't seen my great-uncle Neil since then. Now, fifteen years later, I was about to reunite with him.

The Jesus People decided to send an evangelistic team to Mardi Gras, and I was to lead the group of fifteen people. We had just enough money to get there and found lodging where we could, one time staying in a used furniture store.

Uncle Neil invited me to visit him at his office, not his home. He'd heard about me joining a commune and knew how much it had upset my parents. We had a great visit that day in his office, so much so that he didn't hesitate to invite me to his house the following day to see my aunt. Aunt Joann was his fourth wife and some thirty years younger. She was the age of my parents, and the only one of his wives I ever knew. They both enjoyed meeting my wife, Pegge, and our daughter, Mindy, who was only a year old.

After we left, Uncle Neil called my parents to say, "I don't know what all the concern is about with Neil, Jr. He's turned into a fine young man and has become very responsible with his work." He added, "I would be proud if my grandson was doing as well."

I continued to lead a team to New Orleans every year for the next six years. Evangelism was not my particular gift. I preferred to make sure everyone and everything was alright. Who's cooking? Is everything clean? How are we doing financially? How is everyone doing? What is our daily schedule? Still, one of my most memorable opportunities to witness came during one of these trips. Some of our community members had formed a band called The Resurrection Band, and they traveled to Mardi Gras with us to perform. Uncle Neil came to the concert, which was held in an outdoor concert venue right across the street from Jackson Square. The lead singer, Glenn Kaiser, gave a lengthy sermon at the end of the set and concluded by inviting people forward to commit their life to Christ. I asked my uncle if he wanted to go forward. He shook his head and said, "No." I told him that before I left I wanted to make sure he understood the gospel. He said he would like that.

The next morning I went with Dawn and a few other friends to his house to talk with him. As usual, he dominated the conversation for a good forty-five minutes, until I said, "Uncle Neil, you said you were open to me making the gospel clear to you, so you need to give us a chance to talk."

He said, "Okay," then asked, "Why do you believe in

God?"

Dawn answered with a basic apologetic response. "The world has a design to everything that was made so there must also be a designer."

My uncle seemed intent on listening, and said, "I've always believed in God. I've just never been sure who this Jesus is. But here's the thing. I see in your large group a love that doesn't exist in small families of four or five. So I do believe in Jesus and who you say He is."

At that point, I said, "Uncle Neil, if you believe that Jesus is who He says He is, then you need forgiveness for your sins because that is why Jesus came. Will you pray with me?"

He agreed. I led him in a prayer similar to the one I prayed in the beach house ten years earlier. He began to repeat the prayer after me, but then began his own heartfelt prayer of repentance, saying, "God, You know me. You know the things I've done. Jesus, I ask You to forgive me for those things. I surrender my life to You. Amen."

Not long after, my uncle called my dad and said, "I want you to know that not only do I think the world of Neil, Jr., and respect his life's decisions, but I have also joined rank with him."

The following year, our team went back to New Orleans for the last time. A group of outspoken and obnoxious fundamentalist Christians had destroyed all hopes of us presenting a loving Christian message. They carried huge banners that said, *You're going to hell!* and referred to the Mardi Gras party-goers as "cigarette-sucking sinners." We were trying to witness to others about the love of Jesus but ended up spending much of our time explaining that we weren't part of that group.

I kept in touch with my Uncle Neil throughout the year, sending him stories to encourage him in his faith. I tore chapters from Corrie Ten Boom's book, *Tramp for the Lord,* thinking he wouldn't read a whole book if I sent it to him. When I saw him again that following year, I was amazed at the power the word of God had to bring about change and growth in my uncle's crusty old heart.

The Jesus People continued to find new ways to witness. In 1984, we began hosting our own music festival outside of Chicago in Grayslake, Illinois. The Cornerstone Festival was a direct reflection of the heart and soul of our community, which was to nurture the hearts and minds of Christian young people. Too many festivals were geared toward the musical tastes of older adults. For the sake of kids and young people like ourselves, Cornerstone Festival flipped all of that on its head. The artists were mostly Christian rock-n-roll, heavy metal, rap, and punk rock with an occasional popular artist like Charlie Daniels thrown in. To this day there are Facebook groups where people continue to reminisce about the annual event that lasted for twenty-nine years.

Uncle Neil flew up to attend the first festival in 1984. I made arrangements for him to stay in a nearby hotel, but after the first night, when I went to pick him up, he was standing outside with his bags packed. "Whatever money I'd spend on staying in a hotel, I'll spend on camping equipment to be able to stay out on the grounds with everyone else," he said.

So off we went to Sears and Roebuck to buy a tent, a cot, a sleeping bag, a flashlight, and a chair. He often said that he believed making it to Cornerstone meant that his warranty was good for another year. Due to congestive heart failure, he couldn't attend in 1992, but he was there every year from the time the Cornerstone Festival began until he passed away in September 1992 at age 93.

My aunt asked me to officiate his memorial service, so I told the story of him coming to Christ that afternoon in New Orleans. At one point I looked up to see my dad sitting in the congregation listening to me intently. I couldn't help but wonder if he still believed I was throwing my life away.

– Chapter Seventeen –
I Lived

Life went on. The homeless found shelter, the hungry continued to be fed, the senior citizens continued to be cared for, and groups from various denominations continued to do mission trips to our community to serve the needy. New people arrived both to help and to grow in their relationship with God and others. My two daughters were growing up. And I was about to face the worst bleeding episode of my life.

It would end up being my final stay in a hospital. I was up all night, out of bed every twenty minutes to sit on the portable toilet, losing blood. I kept the ICU nurse busy bringing me new warm towelettes. Even on death's door, exhausting as it was, I still had a bit of modesty about wiping myself. Waking up to a new day lost significance for me; time was marked by the changing of the nurses from one shift to the other. At one point, I remember saying that I wasn't sure I was going to be able to keep going. The nurse said, "Certainly you've thought about that before."

I recoiled like I was being corrected, but simply said, "Yes, of course I have." But this time it felt very real to me, maybe more so because I had a wife and two young daughters. Dawn, who rarely made hospital visits due to her fear of all doctors and hospitals, came to visit me in the ICU.

A good friend, Sarah, later told me, "We were gathered for our writer's meeting and when the news came of your hopelessness setting in, Dawn rose from her seat like a queen rising from her throne, gathered her coat and winter garb, and said to her assistant, 'Sandy, we're going to the hospital to see Neil.'"

Dawn stood by my bed and said, "Neil, you mustn't entertain thoughts of not making it. Who is going to run the ministry if you don't?"

I shed a few tears and geared up for the fight. Perhaps it was my Mount of Transfiguration moment, like when the angels, Moses, and Elijah met with Jesus to encourage Him for the plight He was about to face.

The bleeding began subsiding and I was moved out of ICU to a regular floor. Hospitals prefer not to keep people on public aid in the ICU. The first night in a regular ward was short-lived, as I was soon vomiting blood again and was rushed back down to the ICU as things went from bad to worse. My doctors, Dr. Arvydas Vanagunas and Dr. Robert Craid, were the leaders in the field of gastro-enterology at Northwestern Hospital in Chicago. A new procedure of endoscopy called sclerotherapy was still in a trial period. A scope was put down my throat to look for the varices in my esophagus, but little did they know it would be like poking a pin into a water balloon. I regurgitated blood on them all. I was wheeled quickly into another room where a balloon-like device was inflated in my throat to put pressure on the veins to stop the bleeding. It also made me feel as if I couldn't breathe, so I heaved myself nearly off the table, screaming, "You're killing me!"

I was injected with a sedative and soon went out.

Dr. Vanagunas and Dr. Craig performed the sclero-therapy, which amounted to injecting the veins with a substance that blocked the blood flow by shutting down the vein. The bleeding was so severe that it prevented them from seeing exactly what veins they were injecting. When the procedure was completed, there was no clear indication whether it would be successful.

I awoke hours later. Both doctors were present. They smiled and said, "It's good to see you. It was about a fifty-fifty chance you would pull through." I'm sure my medical history is included in the annals at Northwestern Hospital of early sclerotherapy procedures used to treat esophageal varices. All my previous surgeries had served their pur-pose, but none had offered a permanent cure. I was fortunate to have lived long enough to benefit from these medical advances.

When I returned to the community, I discovered there had been special times of prayer held for me. I was also told that my daughter, Mindy, who was about seven years old, was standing in line for dinner and overheard someone say, "It doesn't look like Neil is going to make it."

Mindy looked the person straight in the eye, and with childlike faith declared, "Yes, he will."

Because I hadn't undergone invasive surgery, my recovery was much quicker, but having lost such an enor-mous amount of blood, I was weak for quite a while. I would continue to have a yearly upper endoscopy to check for developing varicose veins for the next ten years. I was finally told by Dr. Vanagunas, "You are healed." More than thirty years later, I am still without a bleed.

St. Benedict said, "Remember to keep death before

your eyes daily." When I was young, I don't know if I ever entertained the idea that I could die. I just wanted to get through the transfusions so I could go home and jump on the trampoline, ride my bike, and explore the woods down by the river. In reality, death was always before my eyes, not only from my hospitalizations but from the many days I spent roaming the cemetery where my grandmother worked. My parents, of course, lived with the possibility that my time here with them might be brief. We never talked about it. We each just lived it in our own way. For me it was always a matter of something to get beyond. One day I won't. Jesus promised, "I am the resurrection and the life. Whoever believes in me, though he die, yet shall he live" (John 11:25).

I live.

– Chapter Eighteen –
Mamma's Funeral

The Jesus People had been gifted with a piece of property near the Current River in Missouri. We built a ten-bedroom log cabin lodge so our members could take a relaxing break from life in the city. My family and I were vacationing there when I got the call informing me Mamma had passed away. My mind was flooded with the many memories I had of this classy, saintly lady. How blessed I had been to have such a wonderful person in my life.

I told my dad that I wanted to share a few stories about my grandmother at her funeral. It was unusual for someone other than the priest to speak at a Catholic service, but an allowance was made, though I was not invited to speak from the podium. I stepped into the aisle and turned to face the congregation. I began with a story of a discussion my sister, brother, and I had about what we wanted to be when we grew up. After several attempts to outdo each other by naming all the typical occupations, such as a doctor, firefighter, and lawyer, I said, "I want to be like Mamma." At that, the competition ended.

I shared the story I had heard from my cousin, Chris, about my grandmother and her brother, my Great Uncle Neil. Once, when Mamma was visiting her family in New

Orleans, Uncle Neil had a heated exchange with his wife, Joann, in the kitchen in front of Mamma. Her father stormed away and Mamma followed him. Mamma let her brother know that if he didn't apologize for his outburst, even though she had just arrived, she was going to catch the next flight home. A few minutes later, Uncle Neil went back to the kitchen to apologize to his wife, something Chris had never seen him do. Chris said, "Your grandmother had quite the ability to influence others toward right behavior."

—

I told everyone how Mamma's house was decorated by interior designers and filled with beautiful antiques. Whenever I was there, things tended to get broken, and I was there quite a bit as a kid. My grandmother would always say, "No worries. I never really liked that thing anyway." Life went on without whatever priceless treasure I'd managed to destroy.

I ended by telling everyone how Mamma prayed every morning and every night. I was quite sure she carried many of us in her prayers every day. I said, "I don't know if everyone here is a praying person, but I want to encourage you to become one since there will now be an absence of prayer on your behalf from my grandmother."

We left the church to go to the cemetery where Mamma had worked for forty years. Now she was taking her place amongst the many graves. I found it appropriate that our family plot was near the office where she had worked for so many years. A large tent had been set up since rain was in the forecast. Florida rain bursts are sometimes referred to as "frog stranglers"—short and intense. When the downpour came, the attendants used brooms to push the sagging roof of the tent up to make the water run off. Internment services don't usually last long, and before it ended the sun was shining and the wet grass and shrubbery were glistening.

The funeral home director, who was good friends with my grandmother, looked at the sky and asked me, "What do you have to say about all this rain?"

I said, "Scripture says the rain falls on the just and the unjust. I believe we know who it fell on today."

He smiled and said, "I want you to see your grandmother before she is buried." He knew I had missed the viewing the night before, having arrived earlier that day. My daughter Kirsten was too young to fully understand where Mamma had gone, so Pegge and the girls and I stayed behind after everyone left. Getting to view my grandmother's body before it was lowered into the ground helped Kirsten make sense of things. She seemed to understand where Mamma was, and I appreciated a final glance of a life well-lived.

My dad told me that a friend of his often commented, "Your son sure saved that funeral from being just one more rote memorial service." It was my dad's roundabout way of giving me a compliment, which I did appreciate.

– Chapter Nineteen –
Welcomed into the Fold

When I was asked to take on responsibility in the community, I discovered my capacity to care. Who knew that deep within I was a caregiver? My heart of stone needed some major dynamite blasts in order to become a heart of flesh. I was part of a leadership team to provide pastoral care to the community as a whole. My days were spent dealing with daily conflicts and communicating the schedule of events for a group that had grown to more than two hundred people. Our community was evolving from being a group of "shock troops" spreading the gospel to a community of families with children at its center. We began our own home school, an endeavor that eventually grew to include more than a hundred students ranging from Pre-K to 12th grade. We were manning chaplain positions in Cook County Jail and doing volunteer visitations at a few Chicago hospitals. This required us to take courses at North Park Seminary or Moody Bible Institute for certification. Life for everyone was one long learning curve!

We were not the typical expression of a church, since we all lived together in a community. As the community grew, we became a large fish in a small pond, and a desire began to emerge in us to be a large fish in a larger pond.

We began to knock on the doors of some mainstream denominations. There were inherent roadblocks from the beginning for us with some denominations. Most wanted us to become more presentable by cutting our hair and cease playing rock-n-roll music. Basically, they didn't understand our counter-cultural mission. They also failed to under-stand the impact our music group, REZ Band, was having on young people worldwide, oftentimes suggesting certain music styles, namely rock-n-roll, were unchristian.

Eventually, a long-time friend and social justice advocate, John Perkins, suggested we check out the Evangelical Covenant Church (ECC), although he questioned whether we should join a denomination. The ECC may have seemed small when compared to the "big boys" like the Baptists, Lutherans, and Methodists, but at that time it included more than eight hundred churches across the United States and Canada and was a denomination that was increasing in numbers rather than shrinking.

The ECC headquarters was in Chicago, right in our backyard. The members of the executive branch were greatly impressed by our urban outreach to the homeless and low-income senior citizens and were surprised by our abilities to embrace alternative populations that typical churches found difficult to incorporate. Our Cornerstone Festival was now attracting nearly twenty thousand Christians from various affiliations. This four-day music and arts event was home to more than three hundred bands and offered tracts of education to choose from in the morning and afternoon seminars. Some were taught by professors from North Park University and Seminary.

After a two-year courtship, the Evangelical Covenant Church welcomed our community, Jesus People USA, as a member congregation. I was disheartened when I discovered that five churches voted against us joining. When I made mention of it to the current president, Rev. Paul Larsen, he chuckled and said, "I had way more people vote against me."

It was a significant event for our community to join a denomination. As a member church, we were something of an enigma. Many communities that began when we did, in the early seventies, didn't last long for a number of reasons. No doubt, our success was partly due to our evolution from a one-person leadership to a plurality of leaders within the first two years of our existence. We intentionally structured our leadership on a co-pastor basis, each having an equal say, with no one person viewed as the senior pastor. It was our intention to make decisions by consensus, a very slow way of decision making, which in the end is more healthy for community life. Knee-jerk decision-making doesn't bode well for people in general. Each leader had his or her area of specific responsibilities, but we all were accountable and responsible for each other and for decisions that affected the community as a whole. If the kitchen staff wanted to rearrange how the food was stocked, they were free to do so. If they wanted to change the meal times, then that decision had to be discussed at large. No doubt, communication was a constant challenge, and when it was done well, it saved a lot of confusion and anger. We always had plenty of both. As a leadership team, we met daily when we first began and eventually scaled back to once a week. As part of the ECC, the pastors were required to take continuing education courses to maintain our licensure, and ultimately most of the team became ordained to Word and Sacrament, the highest form of credential in the denomination. The denomination factored in our life experiences in Christian service and granted us ordination after completing required classes, instead of having to take the typical four years for our masters of divinity.

Personally, I was delighted and challenged by our new relationship with the ECC. I found my way into golf outings with other pastors and attended the annual gatherings, both local and national. I enjoyed meeting new people and sharing the struggles pastors dealt with in their local church congregations. The community life I lived may have differed from the typical pastor, but problems are problems and we could all relate to each other. Whenever there was an ECC meeting in another part of the country, John would say, "You go. You look the most like them."

At times, I wondered if I aspired to a leadership position for all the wrong reasons. Surely, there were more qualified, naturally-gifted, selfless people than I. No one could have been more naive when it came to the realities of Christian leadership, and for that matter, life in general. I took great comfort in knowing that the disciples of Jesus often got it wrong. Jesus set them straight, and life in community with others helped set me straight. We were committed to being open and honest with each other, and central to our vision was the desire to help others grow and mature in Christ. Both of these matters were essential if we were to stay together. As a pastoral team, we believed we couldn't expect the community to be any healthier than we were as a leadership team. We held each other accountable and learned to be able to speak the truth, in love, to each other.

You have nothing to give to anyone. I could still hear the words my mother said to me the day I left home to join this community. She was right. I had been so sheltered and catered to all my life, what did I know about struggle and hardship? What did I know about grace and kindness? The learning curve was huge for me, but in truth, it was for everyone.

Theologian Eugene Peterson said about life in community, "Nothing requires more attention and energy. It is easier to do almost anything else." Leaving home and moving into a community was the beginning of an education I doubt I could have attained any other way, and I don't regret one minute of it. My parents didn't realize how much they had instilled in me the desire to pursue my dream and respect others. It had simply never had an opportunity to grow, but after years of communal living, the seeds that they and others had planted began to sink in and germinate.

– Chapter Twenty –
Living in a Miracle

The 90s ushered in a decade of incredible growth for the Jesus People. We were now being recognized by other churches, social service agencies, and local officials for our work with Uptown's poor and needy. The first floor of our building on Malden Street was being used around the clock. It was our dining room by day, and each night we replaced the tables and chairs with mattresses for the homeless. The ministry of housing the homeless continued to grow each year, especially during the winter. Our capacity became increasingly limited, and we needed more space.

In the fall of 1989, I attended a service provider meeting in Uptown with the Chicago Commissioner of Human Services, Rev. Daniel Alvarez, Sr. I told him and his assistant, Jackie Edens, how we had welcomed a few single men into our lobby during the freezing winter nights and how our dining room was now being used to house homeless single women and children year-round. The situation was becoming strained, but we had found a building nearby we thought would give us the needed space to continue and expand our services. It was a warehouse for sale on Clifton Street, between Leland and Wilson Avenue, where it became a one-way alley. It was, in fact, nicknamed Murder Alley. Alvarez asked me and fellow community member Chris Ramsey to take him to see the building after the meeting.

We drove the two blocks to the building and peered through the windows of the vacated warehouse. Jackie let us know the city does not give money for the purchase of properties and apologized for not being able to help. As I went to shake hands with the commissioner, he contradicted this by saying, "Get all the paperwork on the building to me by tomorrow morning."

Jackie winked and said, "You should have had it to him yesterday."

The city bent the rules and gave us the down payment of $75,000 to purchase the building with the stipulation that we would run it as a shelter for the next ten years. The purchase was accomplished through the lending arm of the ECC, National Covenant Properties, which carried the mortgage. Joining the denomination had made expansions possible for many of our ministries since National Covenant Properties granted loans to churches when ordinary secular, financial institutions might not.

We now had a large shelter to house the homeless who had been sleeping on the floors in our dining room, but due to our own expansion, we were also in need of more space. We had outgrown the four buildings we owned along Malden and Magnolia Streets.

The following year, a promising building was being sold at auction. The Chelsea Hotel was a ten-story building that had fallen into disrepair. Built in the late twenties, it attracted guests to the "famous Wilson Avenue" and nearby "bathing beaches" for a reasonable rate of two dollars per day. In the late sixties, it became a retirement home for seniors. When the boiler quit working in 1989, the owner declared bankruptcy and left the one hundred and fifty senior citizens who were living there to freeze.

The Alderwoman, Helen Shiller, brought blankets and coats to the residents and even moved into the building along with her staff to care for the seniors until the boiler could be repaired a few weeks later. Shiller was an active proponent of affordable housing. Some called her a socialist for her anti-gentrification stance. She believed that the residents of Uptown deserved to stay there rather than be pushed out by developers. She became a strong force on the political front for much of what our community was able to accomplish.

Were the Jesus People ready to take on a three-hundred-sixty-room building? And not just any building, but a decaying, dilapidated hotel where the outdated plumbing was buried inside twelve-inch-thick cement walls, with three elevators that needed constant maintenance and repairs, and tuckpointing that had to undergo an inspection every five years? The repair costs promised to be astronomical. When my Great Uncle Neil, who had years of construction experience, saw the building he said, "This is the kind of building you give to your enemies."

Whether we knew it or not, a building like the Chelsea Hotel could cause us to go into bankruptcy. I'm not sure if we were foolish or full of faith. It was probably some of both. The possibility of all of us being under one roof seemed inviting, but we weren't the only ones interested in the old hotel. Investors called and offered our community $5,000 to back out of bidding at the auction. We politely told them we were going to take our chances. National Covenant Properties got on board with our plan and gave us a ceiling of 2.2 million dollars to bid. Privately, we had made an offer to buy the building straight out for two million dollars before the auction took place, but it was believed the bidding would bring a higher amount. We arrived at the courtroom with the required certified check for $100,000 in order to make a bid.

The courtroom was packed not only with prospective buyers but with people who were simply interested in the future of Uptown, especially those who owned homes and hoped for gentrification. The judge took his seat and began the auction with an opening bid of $1,750,000. A member of our leadership team, John Herrin, raised his hand and presented the judge with the $100,000 certified check to start the bid. The judge continued the bidding process, but no one responded. The room fell quiet, and then a request was made by some other investors to meet with the judge behind the doors of his chambers.

A Jewish attorney who knew of our community whispered to John, "Are you praying?"

John said, "Yes, and our whole community is praying."

The attorney continued, "Well, you better pray because what is going on in the backroom isn't good. You can be sure they are trying to negotiate with, or bribe, the judge for an extension of the sale."

A few minutes later, the judge resumed his place, banged the gavel on the desk, and announced, "Everyone had the same amount of time to get their finances together to bid on the building, but only one group brought a check. The Chelsea Hotel at 920 West Wilson Ave is sold to Jesus People U.S.A. for $1,750,000."

There was an audible gasp in the room. The attorney said to John Herrin and Tom Cameron, "In all my days of being in courtrooms, I felt an undeniable Presence in this room today." Personally, I found that greatly comforting because, like the children of Israel after crossing the Red Sea, certainly we were unaware of the giants we'd encounter ahead.

It was a mammoth undertaking for all of us to move into this ten-story building over the next couple of years. Moving is high on all stress charts, but I doubt the stress of moving a community of a few hundred people can be measured. Everyone helped with whatever skills they had to assist others with their move. There was some rhyme and reason why some people had to move earlier than others, so in the midst of what seemed like unbelievable chaos, there was a thread of order to be found in it all. I believe God only allows us to see so far down the road because if we saw all that lay ahead, we'd probably turn back. I know from experience that there is a Presence and grace for today, and when tomorrow comes that Presence and grace will be there, too.

Paul Larsen, the president of the ECC at that time, stopped over to see the place. The building hummed with activity. It is quite the challenge to make things look clean and orderly when you live with a few hundred others.

I told him, "We're working on making things more organized."

Paul said, "Oh, don't make it too organized or less gets done."

Turns out, we were the quintessential picture of not being too organized and yet getting an incredible amount of things done each day. We were a living illustration of "living in the midst of a miracle on the edge of disaster."

It was July 1990 when we inherited the responsibility

for the one hundred and fifty senior citizen residents living throughout the ten floors, which meant we had to provide three meals a day and a weekly room cleaning. At that time, we were already preparing meals for the few hundred members of our own community, three meals for those living in the shelter, and an afternoon meal every day for two hundred homeless people. We discovered that the residents were told by the former management that a religious cult was taking over the management of the building and that they had another building for people to move into. Josephine, a nurse for thirty-five years in Chicago, asked Joan, a single woman who had been a legal secretary all her life while caring for her aging parents, "Are you leaving?"

Joan said to Josephine, "No. It can't get any worse." Both of these women happily lived out the remainder of their lives with us. They both became honorary grandmothers in our community.

In time, we also learned that the former management had taken advantage of some of the seniors by collecting rent a couple of times a month from those who had memory problems. Most of the rooms had not been cleaned, which was part of what the renters paid for. Once, while talking with one of the seniors who was sitting on the carpeted steps going into the dining room, I soon discovered the rug was wet under her. As we became familiar with each senior's needs, we realized that almost half of the residents should not have been living independently and needed to be moved into nursing homes. We were able to move the seniors to the top three floors once those floors were renovated. The rooms there were warmer, and the views of the lake were spectacular. The former owner had his living quarters on the ninth floor. The area was now converted into offices and a large multi-purpose room for the senior residents. The picture windows provided a picturesque view of the lake, and the front windows allowed for seeing the lights at Wrigley Field at night.

The Jesus People community lived on the second through seventh floors. The first floor of the old Chelsea Hotel used to be a ballroom back in the day, but now it served as the common area for dining and meal preparation, along with other multi-purpose rooms and offices. There was a room with theater seating and a large screen stocked with old movies and musicals from the 40's and 50's. My daughters loved to go there and both grew up singing old classic movie tunes. There is a double lot adjacent to the building, and when we purchased the building it had a moat-like pool of water in the middle. We had to fill this in to protect the kids. For a few years, the lot looked like war-torn Beirut with kids playing and digging in the dirt. Eventually, a member's family donated the money to put in a big playground, basketball court, and a lovely garden area for the senior citizens to enjoy.

I had to laugh at the small frustrations that tried to derail us. The Chelsea is a 10-story building that had no working intercom system, which made communication near impossible. Cell phones were not a common commodity at the time. There were three landline phones per floor, which no one wanted to answer because it often took five to ten minutes to go search for the person being called, let alone having to take messages. There was the constant sound of a phone ringing on every floor until benevolence grabbed hold of someone's heart, or sheer irritation. This resulted in a momentary reprieve, then the ringing would start up again.

External challenges arose, but as a community, we had made it through enough crises to know that we could get through anything. My faith in God to help us survive and support one another was never stronger.

—

Our common purse now included the services of practically every construction trade known to man. There was a Jesus People porch and deck company, a Jesus People moving company, Jesus People painting company, JP roofing, JP carpentry, JP windows, JP electrical, you name it. We had many community members who became highly skilled in their trades. For years, everyone lived without carrying a dime in their pockets. It sounds crazy for life in the United States, but I've read that this is true for many who lived in convents and monasteries, especially before Vatican II. When someone needed to go to the doctor or needed a token to board the "L" train, they went to the petty cash office to have that need met. As a group, we set aside money for various celebrations, such as birthdays, anniversaries, and vacations. There are always a thousand questions on this topic of finances in community, but I'll limit my answer to, "We just kept making it work."

Occasionally, there were times when we couldn't pay our rent, and I was one of the people who would have to meet with David Johnson, the head of National Covenant Properties to explain the reason for our late payment. He was the stereotypical bean counter with spectacles on his head and an adding machine on his desk. In his no-

nonsense manner, he would give us stern warnings. But our meetings with David always ended with a warm-hearted interest in our ministries. He would ask, "Do you have any stories about the ministry you can tell me?" Who knows, he may have needed some to share with the board of directors he had to answer to, but I can only offer praise for this department, under both David's leadership and his successor, Steve Dawson.

Over the next decade, as the community settled into the Chelsea Hotel and grew to fill the three-hundred-sixty rooms, I collected many stories. One that I never wanted to share was that of my youngest daughter, Kirsten, who had begun a frightening descent into a world of addiction. As I immersed myself in the day-to-day challenges of collaborative leadership with our burgeoning community, I carried an increasing fear that I might one day lose her, one of the brightest lights of my life.

– Chapter Twenty-One –

Under a Microscope

One Sunday morning I woke to discover the Jesus People featured on the front page of the Chicago Tribune. The headline read: *Exodus From Commune Ignites Battle for Souls*; the photo showed me standing waist-deep in a large lake in Bushnell, Illinois, baptizing a young girl during our annual Cornerstone Festival. The article referred to the Jesus People as a "cloistered, inner-city religious commune" that was "hemorrhaging longtime members" and implied that we were proselytizing in order to recruit new people.

The girl in the photo had traveled to the festival with her youth group and had especially waited to be baptized during the event. She did not have any plans to join the Jesus People, nor was I assisting the baptisms that took place there in hopes of anyone to do so. Yet I was struck by the irony of the image. I was doing my part to save a girl I'd never met while, away from the public lens, I was struggling to save my own daughter.

Kirsten, my youngest, was now nearly twenty years old, and her battle with addiction was growing worse. In her early teens, she had developed a severe eating disorder. She was bulimic and anorexic, and before long there was no hiding her emaciation. When our family went to celebrate my parents' fiftieth wedding anniversary, I felt compelled to forewarn them about her appearance. Eventually, Kirsten volunteered to be admitted into a teen treatment program in the suburbs of Chicago and was slightly helped.

But her challenges persisted. Once, when I drove Kirsten to a house where she was cat-sitting, she ran in to feed the cat and when she got back in the car, she smelled like alcohol. Money would come up missing, and even if she was the only one in the room, she would deny it. Pegge and I weren't sure what to do. She was too old for us to ground her.

My daughters were aware that I had left home at eighteen to move into a community. When my oldest daughter, Mindy, turned eighteen and decided to move out, I tried to talk her out of it, but it didn't work. Mindy moved to Seattle, where she sowed her wild oats—at least some of them. A few years later, she moved back to our community and took a teaching job in our community's home school. Later, she began classes at the city college near us and over time graduated with her master's degree in social work from the University of Illinois. She also worked in Alderwoman Helen Shiller's office for a couple of years, which gave her insights into the political aspects of helping underprivileged residents in Uptown. Mindy continues this work in Uptown with Mercy Housing.

Soon Kirsten wanted to get her own apartment too, and what could we do? We helped her find one and paid the deposit. Her mother and I hoped that a move toward independence would provide the confidence she needed to become responsible for her life and hopefully discover sobriety. On my first visit to her new place, I opened the refrigerator to find it mostly empty except for a bottle of wine. I didn't say anything.

Instead, I helped her find a good job in a downtown Chicago film and recording studio, but her instabilities eventually caught up with her. She lost the job when she went to visit some friends in Minneapolis and stayed without giving a two-week notice. Pegge and I kept in touch as best we could with her, but there were times we wouldn't hear from her for weeks on end. We lived in fear that we would get a call saying she had overdosed. Her life continued to spiral out of control, and I could do nothing about it but worry.

And now, on the heels of my own daughters leaving the community, came the Chicago Tribune article reporting that "hundreds have packed their Bibles and their children and their secondhand clothes and left Jesus People USA."

The story focused on several families who had left the community after raising objections about the way we elected our leaders and handled our finances. The articles insinuated a mishandling of the city money we received for our shelter. Our attorney provided clear and detailed documentation of how our income from the city was received and used by the separately incorporated shelter, Cornerstone Community Outreach. Also, a letter supporting the Jesus People community as an upstanding member church of the ECC was sent to the Tribune by ECC president Glenn Palmberg, but neither was printed by the paper.

As typical with articles written about communities, it was a gross mischaracterization of our community and mission. What was described as an "exodus" was an everyday reality of our community life, with people coming and going, and which is fairly common for all churches. The Jesus People traditionally appealed to those who were unstable or searching for purpose.

"Say what you want about us," I told the reporter. "But the fact is we attempt to help the kinds of people the rest of society writes off. We take in the drug addicts and the alcoholics and the sexually confused. We take in the down and out. We give them a home and a family and we love them." Perhaps the article was correct in saying we were in a "battle for souls." In truth, we were trying to fulfill the mission of "welcoming others as Christ had welcomed us."

Not everyone has a good experience living in a community, just as everyone doesn't have a good experience in a church they may visit or a job they may take. There are always those who feel judged or convicted by others' good deeds, and seek to do harm to such people. One person was fond of restating Jesus' comment of "many are called, but few are chosen" by saying, "many are called, but few can stand it." It's common for people to have exaggerated expectations and experience them as unfulfilled, so they leave in hopes of finding what they dream of. In some cases, teens or young adults who have been born into a community become angry with their parents for raising them there. But rather than blame their parents, they blame the community.

Did my daughter Kirsten blame Pegge and me for her upbringing? Were we responsible for her addictions? What could I have done differently? These were the kinds of questions that plagued me. Perhaps the most painful and mystifying question of all, the one that wouldn't leave me, was: is there anything I can do now to save her?

– Chapter Twenty-Two –
My Parents' Declining Health

My parents worried about how to save me from throwing my life away when I joined a commune at eighteen. Now, as a parent, I could more easily relate to the concerns they must have had. From my perspective, the situation with Kirsten seemed far more threatening, since she was speeding down the destructive path of substance abuse. All addictions have their similarities; I had taken drugs at an earlier age, but my drug use would have been considered recreational compared to Kirsten's. I used marijuana as an escape from my depression, and my occasional use of psychedelics was an effort to impress others and gain their acceptance. Kirsten was rounding her thirties with a complete physical dependence on both drugs and alcohol, and I feared we would lose her altogether. After the many weeks and months of worry about her turned into years, I began to face the reality that I was slowly losing both of my parents, as well.

One day, my mother drove to the Publix grocery store, and when she got back in the car, she couldn't remember how to get back to her home less than a mile away. She called my brother to get her, and afterward willingly gave up the keys to her car. My dad had a series of mini-strokes around the same time, which led to the onset of dementia for him as well. He had his driver's license revoked by his physician, but taking away the keys to his car was near impossible. He remained my mother's chauffeur for the remainder of her life, taking her to restaurants and to her weekly beauty parlor appointment.

My sister Jan did the best she could to manage my parent's affairs, but not without resistance from our dad. Once, without forewarning my parents, she showed up with two women she had hired as caregivers for them. My mother befriended the women and was grateful for their help. My dad tolerated them as long as they understood that he saw them only as hired hands. Thankfully, the women were both lovely people who knew how to over-look my dad's racial insults, or maybe they'd simply grown accustomed to the ways of white people in the South.

On one of my trips to Florida, my sister, brother, parents, and I went out to dinner by ourselves, without our spouses or children. I marveled as the five of us sat around the table, knowing this had not happened for three and a half decades. It brought me back to my childhood. And just like back then, my dad and sister had words before leaving the house, so even the tense atmosphere felt familiar. It was customary for at least one person's nose to be out of joint. We ordered and were waiting for our food without much conversation when my mother turned to me and asked, "Did we order yet?"

I said, "Yes."

She said, "Oh. What did I order?"

"The shrimp scampi," I told her.

She smiled and said, "Oh good. I love the shrimp scampi."

A couple of minutes later, my mother turned to me and said, "Did we order yet?"

Again, I said, "Yes."

"What did I order?"

I reminded her for the second time. "The shrimp scampi."

"Oh good." She sighed happily. "I love the shrimp scampi."

Another few minutes went by, and my mother said, "Did we order yet?"

I smiled. "Yes, we ordered, Mother."

"What did I order?"

This time I said, "It will have to be a surprise."

"Oh good," she said. "I love surprises!" There were no more questions after that.

My dad was not so easily placated. I went with him to the bank one afternoon to cash the weekly check he received from the cemetery. Inside, we waited our turn to see the teller. He handed the woman the check and said, "I'd like three, three, and three."

The woman politely said, "How would you like the cash, sir?"

Again, my dad said, "I want three, three, and three."

"Three what, sir?"

My dad's temper was starting to rise. "I want three, three, and three."

"I don't understand, sir. Three what?"

A supervisor stepped in to try to calm the situation, which made my dad all the more irritated.

I stepped forward and calmly said, "Dad, they don't understand what three, three, and three means." I was quickly dismissed with a few curse words as the security guard moved closer to the situation. I finally got my dad to leave the bank, thinking that we had narrowly escaped without being arrested or shot. He was dumbfounded that no one in the bank understood English. When I told my brother and sister about the incident, they were so pleased that I got to experience what they dealt with every day.

The following morning, I was sitting in the living room area when my parents finally emerged from their bedroom dressed for the day. Just as they were exiting the room, my dad told my mother to come back to the bathroom because she hadn't brushed her teeth.

She replied, "I don't want to."

My dad is extremely meticulous to the point of exhibiting obsessive-compulsive disorder, especially over hygienic matters. He said, "Janice, you have to brush your teeth."

My mother may have had dementia, but she still knew how to push my dad's buttons and persisted to protest, saying, "But I don't want to."

This angered my dad all the more. My mother finally conceded and said, "See, this is the problem of life. Everyone is always trying to make you do what you don't want to do."

All of life had just been summed up into one succinct sentence by my mother, in spite of her dementia.

A few hours later, my mother asked my dad, "Where are we going for lunch?" Obviously, she was getting hungry, and knew to start asking about it early due to the excessive amount of time my dad needed to get ready.

My dad answered, "The watermelon."

"The watermelon?"

My dad persisted, "Yes, to the watermelon."

"Well, that doesn't make any sense!" she said.

"Dammit! We're going to the watermelon."

My mother looked at me and said, "Don't worry about it. We'll figure it out once we get in the car."

I'd already made it clear to my dad that while I was there I would do all the driving or we weren't going anywhere. He pointed out the directions to me as we drove along, happily assuming the role of passenger seat driver. We ended up at their often-frequented restaurant called River City, which is on the water of the St. Johns River. Who knew the River City restaurant was nicknamed the Watermelon?

—

My mom was my first love. She was the sweetest and most beautiful lady I've ever known, and I always wondered with a bit of jealousy how my dad was lucky enough to get such a catch. When she was diagnosed with a rare form of lung cancer and became bedridden, I knew I didn't have much time left with her. She had decided a year earlier not to spend her remaining time sitting in a waiting room at Mayo Clinic and let life take its course. She was at home receiving twenty-four-hour care. I had visited two months earlier and was grateful to return the day before she passed. I went straight to the front room, now turned into her bedroom. I reached out and held her hand, but she quickly pulled it away. Then she opened her eyes, saw it was me, and let me hold it. When I left the room I called my older daughter Mindy, who has a special gift of being present and compassionate, and cried.

The next evening, the whole family went out to dinner.

When we returned, we discovered my mother was greatly agitated and fighting for every breath. My sense was she was annoyed with us for taking so long and had been waiting for us to return. She seemed to let go of her irritation once we were there, and resumed her fight to breathe. As I held her frail hand, one of her beautiful blue eyes opened a little.

I said aloud, in front of everyone, "Mom, you were a wonderful mother, and I am so thankful for all that you did for me my whole life. You were the world's best Southern cook. I want you to know it's okay to go when you're ready. I love you so much."

Everyone followed suit and took a turn to offer their sentiments. My dad didn't speak.

I said, "Dad, do you want to say something? Mom probably needs you to tell her it's okay for her to go."

Though suffering his own battle with dementia, he tearfully said, "Janice, I love you. I have always loved you." Hesitantly, he concluded, "You can go."

Within an hour, she passed.

—

I was asked to give the eulogy at my mother's funeral. The service was held at San Jose Episcopal Church, where I went to school for eight years as a child. I had served there as an acolyte and sung in the choir, once performing a duet with a girl whose voice overpowered mine to the point that no one heard me singing. My sister, my brother, and I were all baptized there. I read scripture there at my brother's and sister's weddings. My mom was a member of the "Daughters of the King," taking her turn each month to iron the vestments for the priest and arrange the flowers for the altar. For eight years I walked to school there, unless it was raining or cold, then my dad would drop the three of us off after a ride that was usually tense since we were slow about getting in the car, making him late for work. I can still hear the squealing tires as we drove into the circle drive, alerting everyone within ear-shot that the Taylor children had indeed arrived.

I was a bit nervous standing before such a large crowd of long-time family and friends, even though I've done it for years as a pastor with my own community. When it was my turn to speak, as I approached the altar to ascend the lectern, I gently laid my hand on my mother's casket and felt my heart heave. I stood silent for a minute catching my breath and calming my emotions before beginning to speak. It is not uncommon for me to pause before speaking, oftentimes leaving the congregation wondering if I have anything to say. I broke the silence with the words of the Apostle Paul in what is the greatest exposition on the subject of love: "And now these three remain: faith, hope, and love. But the greatest of these is love" (1 Corinthians 13:13).

In all my years, my parents never wavered in main-taining these three things for me. My mother lived faith, held on to hope, and demonstrated love. And she didn't do it only for me. Her long-time friend, traveling companion, and stock investor stopped over to pay her respects the day before my mother passed. When I walked Carol to her car, I asked, "How would you describe my mother?"

She said, "Your mother was one of the sweetest and most beautiful people I've ever known. In all the years I have known your mother and traveled with her and spent time with her, I never heard your mother say one unkind word about anyone." She paused for a moment, then added, "When I consider my own character deficits, I look for those who can be role models for me. Your mother was one of those people and always will be."

The next day, my brother and I were at the San Jose Country Club. The former golf pro, Nick, approached me and said, "I'm sorry to hear about your mother. I must tell you, for all the years I knew her, I never heard her say one unkind thing about anyone."

While I cherished these accounts of my mother, there was one memory I held especially dear. During one of our visits to Florida, Pegge and I took my parents to Red Lobster, where my mother ordered her favorite—an appetizer of the mini pizza with lobster. After dinner, she said she wanted to introduce me to the hostess, who was a friend of hers.

"This is my preacher son," my mother said.

When the woman found out that I lived in Chicago, she said, "What on earth made you move north?" Moving north to a southerner is a possible sign of being disturbed. The woman moved on and wasn't really expecting an answer, so I didn't bother giving one.

But my mother grabbed my arm and whispered to me, "It was a calling."

I nearly stumbled, wondering how and when my mother had arrived at such a conclusion. A *calling* seemed like a foreign word in my Episcopal upbringing. I knew my mother had accepted the matter of my life decisions, but those words from her that night as we left the Red Lobster will always remain. They didn't only convey acceptance, but understanding.

– Chapter Twenty-Three –
Dad Likes Me

The year my mother died, my family made plans to spend Christmas with my dad in Florida. I drove down alone a couple of weeks early. Pegge, Mindy, and Kirsten would fly down later. Kirsten came and went from our lives; at this point, she was living in New York and wanted to join us for the holidays. I was grateful but had learned not to cling too tightly to the hope that she had stopped drinking.

I arrived at my parents' home on one of those warm, bright December days you expect in Florida. Inside, I discovered my dad sitting in his recliner with all the shades pulled, staring at a blank television screen. I opened the blinds, saying, "Dad, you're missing the beautiful view of the river on such a fantastic day!"

One of his healthcare helpers, Cynthia, said, "Oh, he likes the shades drawn."

Cynthia was the afternoon caretaker, and as soon as I arrived, his overnight helper quit, leaving me to jump straight into that role. Cynthia told me my dad went to the Stonewood restaurant every night for dinner. Part of her routine was to take him there at the end of her shift, while she waited in the car for him.

When I was a kid, there was always some kind of tension when we went out to dinner as a family. The food was not hot enough. The steak was too rare or overdone. The air conditioning was too cold or there wasn't enough. When Dad was being seated by the hostess, he would always look up at the ceiling to see where the vents were aimed. He hated cold air hitting him. The person seating us had no idea what he was looking at and would begin to look up at the ceiling as well, as if it was about to fall in.

Dad was now even more cantankerous. If his favorite booth was taken, he didn't hide his disgust. Sometimes he'd even sail past the hostess and tell the people in the booth to move while they were in the middle of their dinner. The Stonewood staff learned not to seat anyone at that booth between six and seven every night. They also knew exactly what he would order, which was fortunate since his ability to communicate had become greatly diminished by his dementia.

The conversation was always the same:

"Good evening, Mr. Taylor."

No response from my dad.

"What sounds good this evening?"

No response from my dad.

"The filet mignon?"

A nod.

"Medium rare?"

Another slight nod from Dad.

"Will you be having the baked potato with sour cream and butter?"

Nod.

"And what would you like for a vegetable? The creamed spinach?"

Nod.

"And will you be having blue cheese on the salad?"

Nod.

His order was complete without him ever saying a word.

I had somewhat of a grasp on my dad's routines before my wife and daughters flew in. I also had time to make sure there was no alcohol in his house before they arrived. There was a bar filled with bottles of wine, so I asked the housekeeper to remove them all. I believe she threw them in the garbage. My brother Mark discovered them missing and thought she must have stolen them. He said they were expensive bottles of wine. I confessed that I had told her to throw them away since Kirsten was coming. No crying over spilled wine.

Of course, my efforts to remove temptation had little effect on Kirsten. The roller coaster began before she got there. Her flight from New York was held over in Atlanta due to inclement weather and she missed her connection because she was in the airport bar. Somehow, by the grace of God, she arrived the following day. During her stay, she still went out to drink, and though she thought she was hiding it well, it was obvious to all.

One night, we were out for dinner with my sister Jan and her family. Kirsten excused herself to use the bathroom. Jan was watching her carefully and quietly pointed out to me that Kirsten stopped at the bar first. She had already ordered a drink at the table and was likely taking another one into the bathroom. Jan's awareness of Kirsten made me wonder about the way addiction runs in families; I knew that Jan herself was a high-functioning alcoholic. Jan was athletic and fit. She ran marathons and was careful about what she ate, almost to the point of being anorexic. She did not order a drink with dinner because she drank alone, in private. Her drinking started at nine or ten in the morning and lasted all day, while Kirsten's usually began in the evening or late afternoon.

Jan had a special needs daughter and did her best to care for our dad when his caretakers got sick, or had their own family emergencies, or quit. It wasn't the same as finding caretakers for my mother, who had been sweet and appreciative. Dad fought tooth and nail to maintain his independence and was not grateful, which added even more stress on Jan. More than one caretaker quit. Like Dad, Jan had a volatile temperament and a predisposition to depression. She loved Dad, but the fuse was very short between them. As a result, she wanted to put him into assisted living as soon as possible. For my peace of mind and because I was there to help, I extended my stay to assess whether he really needed to move into a facility.

I met with my brother Mark one afternoon at a nearby Starbucks in the Lakewood shopping area. My brother liked to joke that Starbucks' stock went up whenever I was in town. Mark and I had not spent much time together since I'd left Jacksonville, but we were always able to be at home with each other and engage in genuine conversations. Over coffee, he confessed, "I don't believe Dad really likes me."

I laughed and said, "Mark, if Dad doesn't like someone, it's me. I'm the one who left home, and he has repeatedly said to me, 'You ruined everything.'"

Mark continued, "He doesn't ever seem happy to see me, and mostly when I visit him the atmosphere feels tense."

"Tension is the normal atmosphere around Dad," I said, "Plus, he's in full-blown depression now that Mother is no longer here. Just the other day he told me how Mother had gone and ruined everything."

Dad believed that I was ruining his independence by trying to take his car keys away from him. Neighbors often called to let us know when they saw him driving. I don't know how the neighbors knew he wasn't supposed to drive. We'd been told that, by law, we could be held accountable if he were in an accident, but no one had the guts to take the car away from him. He begrudgingly agreed to let me drive whenever we went anywhere, but would only give me the keys to his Lincoln Town Car after we had gotten in the car. He was always careful to get them back. His acute awareness about the car keys made me wonder about the extent of his dementia.

One night, he forgot to ask me for the keys. I quickly devised a plan to go to a locksmith the next morning to get my own set made. I also planned to make it so that his keys would not work. At two a.m., I was awakened by my dad's heavy footsteps coming down the hallway towards my bedroom. The door opened with his foreboding, large body silhouetted in the door frame. Alarmed, I kept the covers pulled up despite breaking out in a sweat.

"Dad, what do you need?"

He stood there and said, "Well!"

I said, "Well, what?"

He repeated himself, "Well!" He either could not articulate what he wanted to say, or he forgot why he had come to my room.

Finally, I said, "We can talk about it in the morning. You need to go back to bed."

He cooperated, which was completely uncharacteristic of him. I laid there feeling like I was a little boy again, afraid of my dad's temper. He was never physically abusive but, both verbally and with body language, he could scare the bejeebers out of you. I dashed out the next morning to the locksmith and came back with a Starbucks in hand. I told my dad that I'd run out for a coffee and offered his keys back to him as if I had forgotten to give them to him the night before.

A few days later, he said to his daytime helper, "My car keys aren't working." I have no idea when he figured it out, but I did know that it was time to make a decision about his need for care. I ended up staying with him for five weeks, and after seeing him day in and day out, I was convinced he could no longer live alone, even with helpers. He would often ask where the bathrooms were and, once, he absentmindedly almost drank a bottle of dish soap from under the kitchen sink. Plus, I knew the stress was too much for my sister to manage any inconsistencies with the helpers.

Jan and I looked at various assisted living situations in Jacksonville. There were some beautiful places on the ocean. Jan, Mark, and I took dad to see a two-room condominium with a great view of the Atlantic Ocean on one side and a golf course on the other. It had an Olympic-size swimming pool, which Dad would never use. After our tour, he had to sit through an interview and answer questions to test his mental acumen. What year were you born? Who is the current president of the United States? What year is it? What day is it today?

As we were walking out to get in the car, my sister said, "He didn't answer one damn question!"

"He didn't?" I asked surprisingly.

Jan said, "No, we answered them all for him."

I laughed and said, "Well, how did we do?"

Jan and I continued to scour the Jacksonville area and finally found a facility that was newly constructed. It was very clean and didn't have the typical odor of a nursing home. The meals were home-cooked, and the staff was very kind and caring to all the residents. The one drawback was that it wasn't in an upscale neighborhood, nor did it have an ocean view, which didn't sit well with my brother. But Jan and I convinced Mark to come see what the place was like and afterward he agreed that it was a good choice.

We made the necessary arrangements. Jan and her husband decorated his new room and brought furniture in, but when the day came for dad to officially move in, I was left to do it by myself. Mark was away on a golf trip with friends and Jan could not handle going with me, which was probably best since Dad was prone to argue with her the most. After lunch at the nursing home, I walked him to his room where he was surprised to find his furniture. I told him he had to get some therapy for his leg so he would need to stay there for a while. He was not happy and as I was leaving the room, he hit the wall with his fist as hard as he could. I drove away in tears.

I called my brother and sister and sobbed.

Mark said, "If it doesn't work, we'll bring him back home."

But that wasn't really an option unless Mark was going to quit his job. It was beyond Jan to manage his care any longer, and I needed to return to my community.

I was advised not to return for a few days to visit. When I called the next day to see how he was doing, I was told that he found one of the assistants, Fred, to take him to the dining room to eat breakfast. Still feeling like I had betrayed him, I went to the beach to spend the day by myself. Perhaps some people are more prepared for this than I was. For me, it was an absolute surprise to find myself in the role of having to be the parent to the parent.

Over the next six years, I flew to Florida every few months to see him. It gave me a chance to visit with my siblings and their families, play a couple of rounds of golf with my brother, and enjoy getting out of the Chicago winters. The assisted living facility was only five minutes away from where Mark worked, so he was able to stop by during his lunch break, often bringing Dad a milkshake. My dad had always been as healthy as a horse, but eventually, dementia affected his ability to stay in good shape. On nice days, Mark would push Dad in his wheelchair into the sunlight and pretend that Dad was giving him advice over his golf swing. Mark would talk aloud, giving himself the advice that Dad might say, or at least what Mark would have wanted him to say, like, "Great swing. Perfect shot."

How strange that a man who had been a licensed CPA and the senior partner of his law firm, representing well-known people like singer James Brown and the owner of the hotel chain Howard Johnson, who was a leading expert in maritime law giving legal advice to the offshore casinos near Chicago, was now barely able to put two words together. It wasn't long before he began to forget who any of his children were. Still, he was a hero to many, especially to me.

The night we spent together just before he moved into the assisted living facility remains a special memory for me. After Dad went to get ready for bed, which took at least an hour, he came out of his room with his pajamas over his clothes. He stood at a distance in the den, looking at me, daring me to say something about it.

I said, "Well, Dad, you put your pajamas on over your clothes. That's fine with me, but I don't want to wear my pajamas over my clothes to bed."

He remained resolute about his decision and waited for me to accompany him to the bedroom. There was an exact science for getting my dad into bed. The throw pillows had to be placed just so on a nearby chair, the bedspread folded and draped on another, and the blanket and sheets turned down so he could slip under them easily. I'd tuck him into bed with a goodnight kiss on the forehead. When I got to the door, I'd turn the light off and pronounce a kind of benediction: "Goodnight. Sweet dreams."

But on this night, as I was reaching for the light switch, he said, in his gruff way, "Hey!"

"Yes, Dad?"

He said, "I like you." Not *I love you* but *I like you.* Maybe it was his dementia affecting him. All I knew was that hearing "I like you!" had a greater impact on me than "I love you." I never doubted my dad's love for me but, just like my brother Mark, I had doubted whether or not he liked me.

When I met Mark a couple of days later at Starbucks, I announced with great confidence, "Dad likes us!"

– Chapter Twenty-Four –
Saying Goodbye

Did Kirsten wonder if she was liked? For me, learning to love and like myself was an ongoing process. I believed I was born into a world where others wanted and loved me, but in my teenage years, I had succumbed to believing the opposite. I'm sure Kirsten waged a battle similar to my own, where you begin questioning whether you are a good person with bad problems or just a bad person. She'd often comment that people were better off not knowing her since she brought so much chaos wherever she went. Whenever I reached my boiling point with Kirsten's crazy behavior, my mentor and friend Dawn, bless her heart, would say, "When you make the choice to accept and act lovingly towards her, it's just like putting money in the bank." I thought surely I must be a zillionaire.

As each year passed and Kirsten's addictions went from bad to worse, my own sense of isolation and alone-ness felt insufferable. No one wants others to know their daughter is lost in a world of addictions, but living with a few hundred others makes privacy impossible. Communes have the same dynamic as living in a small town but on steroids. There are always words that sting from well-meaning friends. A close friend once said, "No wonder Kirsten is the way she is. You have way more pictures of

Mindy on the wall than of her." It is a terrible pain knowing that others are scrutinizing you when one of your children goes awry. Most were polite enough not to bring her up, though that was also painful. It was a no-win situation. I often tried to let my family in Florida and Pegge's mother and sisters know that Kirsten wasn't doing well. I was really afraid she was going to show up dead one day and didn't want them to be completely unaware of how serious her issues were.

Yet, even in the worst moments, every parent wants to believe things aren't as bad as they are. The smallest positive sign could wipe out all the previous craziness and transport me to a La-la land reality where everything was wonderful and she was doing great. And I wasn't the only one in La-la land. After living with a number of different men, Kirsten once told Pegge that she had always maintained her virginity.

I said, "If she believes that, she has absolutely gone over the brink into insanity. Or if we believe it, then maybe we have."

My training in spiritual direction deepened my sense of God's presence, especially in my relationship with Kirsten. I often talked to God while driving. One day, I sensed God saying to me, "Release your hold on me."

I repeated it back. "Release my hold on you?"

As usual, God did not need to repeat Himself. I just needed to pay attention to what I heard. As I pondered these words, I had an image of me squeezing God so tightly that He couldn't breathe. I didn't know how to let go.

One of the exercises in my spiritual direction training was to practice five minutes of silence. The instructions were to be quiet and simply be open to God speaking something to your heart. As soon as the five minutes of silence began, I sensed God saying, "I've got you." I stayed with that for the whole five minutes. I realized it wasn't God who couldn't breathe. If I could just stop holding on so tightly out of fear and worry, I would be the one who would be able to breathe. Again, I didn't know how to let go.

A couple who attended our church stopped me one morning to tell me a painful story about their son. He had been molested when he was young by a man the couple had welcomed into their home. Their guilt about the molestation nearly destroyed the couple's marriage. The wife began to suffer from severe insomnia, which ultimately caused her husband to lose his executive position in the bank where he worked. Their son spent years on a destructive path but, eventually, he turned his life around and was thriving in a position as a youth pastor. The church was very supportive of the young man.

As I listened to the story, the woman said to me, "You have no idea what it was like to live through all of that." Then she looked me straight in the eye and said, "Wait. You do understand."

I don't know what she saw in my eyes. But it was true, I did understand. Hearing the story tended to depress me at first, but later I interpreted it as an offering of hope for my own situation. As we parted ways, I felt both joy and envy—joy over the return of their son, and envy because I wished the story was mine.

After a long absence, Kirsten reappeared. She returned home after living with some friends in New York. She stayed with Pegge and me for a couple of months. She actually engaged with the community as part of the afternoon kitchen crew. In spite of her addictions, Kirsten was always a good worker.

Hoping that the worst was behind her, I suggested a family outing. The four of us drove to the festival grounds owned by our community in downstate Illinois for a long weekend together. On the four-hour trip back to Chicago, we stopped in Princeton, Illinois to have lunch at a Culver's. While we were eating, a young guy came in and, unbeknownst to me, Kirsten made eye contact with him. There was no conversation between them and the only one to realize the brief connection was Kirsten's sister, Mindy, who never missed seeing something.

Shortly after we returned to Chicago, Mindy was scheduled to stand up in a wedding for a friend of hers. When she attended the wedding rehearsal, she discovered that the guy who had been at the Culver's was one of the groomsmen. He had been driving from Omaha and happened to stop at the same Culver's in Princeton. Unfortunately, Mindy let Kirsten know about this strange coincidence and, over the weekend, Kirsten and the guy, who was named Tyler, met up late one night.

The following Monday, I was golfing at the nine-hole golf course along Lake Michigan. The Marovitz golf course is the inner city's equivalent of Pebble Beach. For some people, golf brings out their worst tempers, but I often went there to enjoy the outdoors and de-stress. Poor shots are frustrating, but that day I was having few frustrations.

I was on the seventh hole when I received a phone call from my wife.

"Kirsten is leaving to go to Omaha with the guy she met over the weekend," she said with a sense of desperation. "If you want to say goodbye, you better come home now."

I was being asked to get back on the roller coaster with my daughter but knew I shouldn't do it. I told Pegge, "I'm not coming home to say goodbye," and ended the call.

It's said that golf is a mental game and from that point on my game fell apart. I triple-bogeyed my next couple of holes, ruining my round. I'm sure the people I was playing with, all strangers, wondered what had happened on that phone call.

Before I went home, I went for a walk and called Dawn. At this point, she and her second husband Curt spent much of their time in Bushnell, where the cell phone connection is intermittent.

I was on Wilson Avenue near Lake Shore Drive, and when I heard Dawn's voice I burst into tears. I had had such hope that Kirsten would turn a corner in her life, and in a moment's notice it all washed out from under me. As I cried, I eventually realized that the call with Dawn had dropped. I was wailing to no one on the other end. Dawn had only caught the beginning of my sobbing and was desperately trying to redial me. When we did manage to reconnect, she listened and ended our conversation by offering a prayer.

The following day, I attended my weekly Tuesday leadership meeting, then retreated to my room on the second floor. I shut the door and locked it. There wasn't a closet for me to crawl in to pray. Instead, I fell on my knees in front of a small trunk that served as our coffee table.

"I can't go on any longer," I told God. I felt the weight of all the years I had spent hoping for Kirsten to make better choices. I wondered what it would be like to yell, as Job did, 'If this is a game you're playing, then you're not much of a God! I don't need you and I don't want you!' But I was too exhausted. The words wouldn't come.

I'm not sure how long I knelt there in silence and despair. It is the greatest pain to watch your child go down a destructive path and be powerless to do anything about it. I had thought that following Jesus would somehow spare me from this kind of pain. I felt like a teenager again, on my knees, willing myself to be happy but not knowing how. I heard my mother telling my teenage self that I had nothing to offer. She was right. I foolishly thought I could learn. I had devoted my life to trying to follow Jesus, to serve my community, to be a good pastor and a loving parent. But the pain of losing my daughter masked any of my accomplishments. I was spent.

How could I let go of my child when I didn't want to?

– Chapter Twenty-Five –
Don't Give up Swimming

Still kneeling by the trunk in my room, I sensed God speak in the familiar way He does with me. It's not audible, but unmistakable. It came as a whisper to my heart, "Don't give up swimming."

It was so clear, I repeated it aloud. "Don't give up swimming." This was the answer to my prayer?

To be honest, I knew immediately what God was saying. He didn't need to repeat Himself. I swam two or three times a week with my friend Dave. We'd often ride our bikes to the pool on nice days, taking our breakfast with us to enjoy on the patio of the Starbucks across the street from Gill Park. Dave was European and liked to joke that his dream as a young person had been to grow up and sit outside at a cafe drinking coffee and reading the paper. In part, it was somewhat realized. It was such a wonderfully simple ambition for such a smart, accomplished person. But as much as I loved swimming, I'd begun to feel guilty enjoying any part of life when my daughter was lost in a world of chaos and instability.

"Don't give up swimming" was God's way of telling me to keep going. In other words, don't throw in the towel. A poem by Denise Levertov called *The Avowal* sums up my own experience in the pool:

As swimmers dare
To lie face to the sky
And water bears them,
As hawks rest upon air,
And air sustains them,
So would I learn to attain
Freefall, and float
Into Creator Spirit's deep embrace,
Knowing no effort earns
That all-surrounding grace.

Kirsten didn't return to Chicago. She and Tyler moved into a studio apartment in a sketchy section of downtown Omaha—not that the surroundings would have bothered her. She'd grown up in the Uptown neighborhood of Chicago well before any gentrification took place. But she did complain about her lack of transportation. The Omaha public transit system is nothing like the CTA. Tyler, who was a lighting technician, spent a lot of time on the road, leaving Kirsten alone. Her longing for independence became overshadowed by loneliness. It was surprising to me for her to call and ask for grocery money. Of course, I would send it.

Eventually, she began cooking and providing part-time care for a senior in her building. The poor old guy had issues with incontinence, so caring for him was more than just cooking. Ironically, we fell into more regular communication due to the isolation she was feeling. I didn't know much about Tyler but guessed that whatever issues he might have were obscured by Kirsten's. One thing was certain: she seemed committed to making it work with him and was well-liked by his family, who all lived in Omaha. Pegge and I drove there on Thanksgiving one year to visit and had dinner with the Packett family. Out of earshot from the rest of the family, Tyler's grandmother said, "We love Kirsten but don't really approve of her and Tyler living together. What about you?"

I said, "Well, to be honest, neither of them asked me." Tyler's grandfather chuckled at my answer.

A couple of years passed until, one day in 2011, Kirsten called me and said, "I need you to help me. Unless I do something about my current situation, I'm going to lose everything I'm trying to hold onto."

Rather than saying, "Yes, I've been telling you that for years," I said, "How would you like me to help you?" I had finally realized that I was not in the driver's seat with her or with God. I'd learned to let go.

"I need you to pick me up and then for you and Mom to help me find a residential treatment program."

Kirsten told me she had attended an Alcoholics Anonymous meeting in Omaha. Like many people, she believed she could outsmart her addiction by learning to drink responsibly. A woman said to her after a meeting, "You know, honey, I honestly think you're really one of us." By "one of us" she meant that Kirsten needed to begin with the first step: admitting she was powerless over alcohol. But Kirsten had never taken that step of surrender. Now, at thirty years old, she was finally asking for help.

Thanks to an inheritance I'd received from my mother, it was possible to arrange a month-long stay at the Hazelden addiction treatment center near Minneapolis. Pegge and I drove to Omaha to get Kirsten, then drove her back to Chicago for her flight to Minneapolis. We had already experienced her missing flights by ending up in an airport lounge, so it was on a wing and prayer that we sent her off. When the time came for family members to be involved in her treatment, we opted to send her boyfriend Tyler. For me, it was a further letting go. Kirsten's recovery was entirely on her.

During one of our phone calls, she complained that many of the classes at Hazelden were focused on relapse, which she said she had no intention of doing. When her month was over, she returned to Omaha and immediately connected with a twelve-step group there, the Valley Hope.

Only one week had passed before I received a phone call late at night from an Omaha police station. Kirsten had been arrested at a bar for disturbing the peace, and they needed two hundred and fifty dollars in cash to bail her out. I told them I lived in Chicago and offered to pay with a credit card. It had to be paid in cash and Tyler was out of town.

"Is she safe?" I asked. The officer said she was. I told the officer that we'd work something out the next day. I prayed the well-practiced serenity prayer and fell back asleep, unlike my wife, who stayed up for hours. Recovery was in Kirsten's court, not mine. I had overcome my chronic anxiety and knew worry did nothing to help her or me. A good night's sleep, nine holes of golf, or a morning swim resembled faith more to me than stress and worry.

The next morning, Kirsten sent a text saying she was at work. I didn't need to know what happened. Instead, I kept to my routine of swimming and took the day off to enjoy the nice weather. I sat outside in our garden, read a book, drank coffee, and enjoyed conversation with some friends.

The next day, Kirsten called and said, "Dad, you never even texted me."

I said, "I know. I had to take care of myself."

I learned that she had called her boss, an older man who was a former alcoholic. He paid the bail, and she went straight to work the same day.

She said, "After work, I drove back to the bar. It was five minutes to seven. I knew the twelve-step meeting started at seven and I wouldn't get there on time. I hate being late. I went anyway. When it was my turn to share, I told everyone about my night in jail. They seemed surprised that the Hazelden girl, as they refer to me, fell off the wagon. But when I was done sharing, an amazing thing happened. Everyone thanked me. I've never experienced being thanked for making a complete mess." Kirsten learned a fundamental lesson regarding relapse, that relapse is a part of recovery, and you must go back to the meetings.

When Kirsten appeared in court, she was sentenced by a judge to attend two meetings a day for the next six weeks. She returned at the end of the six weeks with her attendance card in hand to stand before the judge again. He took her case last, after the room was cleared.

He said, "Congratulations, young woman. You have made it to the sixtieth percentile of those who remain sober. I'd like to ask your permission to give you an additional six weeks because then you will be in the ninetieth percentile of those who maintain sobriety."

Kirsten agreed.

Before we hung up, I said, "Sweetheart, the biggest miracle wasn't the six weeks of sobriety. The bigger miracle was you telling the judge yes."

– Chapter Twenty-Six –
Dodging Arrows

More than forty years had passed since I showed up, uninvited, at a run-down rental house in Gainesville, Florida to join a small, rag-tag group of Jesus followers. On my first night there I met the group's leaders, Dawn and John Herrin. Dawn in particular was the vision-holder for the community. Her clarity of purpose included evangelism and outreach and demonstrating the love of Christ through feeding the hungry and housing the indigent; it was the glue that held our group together. If our goal had simply been to live together, we would have failed. Life in community is for the birds unless there is a purpose bigger than simply living together. Dawn's clear vision of serving God and others, especially the poor, was the essential purpose that held us together. She guided the community. She also guided me, as a friend and mentor, through the most turbulent times with my daughter Kirsten.

Changes can be hard to notice when you are in the midst of living life with others, but some are hard to ignore. A few of my oldest friends and fellow leadership team members were moving on. It was hard for me to imagine anyone doing so after such a long period of life with others. Tom Cameron, a long-time co-pastor, and his wife Janet sensed God leading them to move near their daughter, who was expecting twins. Ron and Marguerite Brown were aging and felt the need for more space. They also longed to be near their children and grandchildren, too. Ron and I had been joined at the hip for thirty years doing the same job and sharing the same office. His absence made me feel like I had become an amputee.

Dawn had been diagnosed with emphysema five years earlier, though she had never smoked a day in her life. She was always quick to encourage others whenever they were ill to see a doctor. This was her one point of hypocrisy because she herself would hardly ever go. She was like an aunt of mine who finally went to see a doctor and died two weeks later from cancer.

Dawn and her first husband John had divorced many years earlier, and she lived as a single person for nearly twenty years. She once told me that she had reached out to hold her own hand in the middle of the night. But being single meant she was able to be more present to everyone in the community, especially me. She once said, "You are the friend who is always there when you don't want a friend around." I took it as a compliment, although it could have meant something different.

When an older man named Curt moved into the community with his teenage daughter, Dawn met her match and the two married. Curt was both a writer and a poet. The two of them knew how to enjoy life to the fullest. Curt suffered from heart problems and Dawn from lung issues. They'd often say that between the two of them they made one very healthy person. As Dawn's breathing became more labored, it became necessary for her to use a walker and soon a wheelchair. Curt became Dawn's caretaker extraordinaire, and they both remained important members of the community.

When Dawn's eightieth birthday neared, one of the residents, Ephraim, mentioned to me that we couldn't let it pass without a celebration. Ephraim was a favorite of Dawn's. Ephraim and his father were true American hobos. From the time Ephraim was young, he and his father jumped trains together to travel across the states. When Ephraim was older, he came to our dinner program for the homeless and ended up finding a home with us. He was put in charge of the dinner guest program, hosting meals for a couple of hundred homeless people each day.

When I made the announcement during a church service that we were having a birthday celebration for Dawn, everyone cheered. I had no idea at the time that this would be a cause for concern with some members of Dawn's family feeling it might be too much for her. Curt weighed in on the decision. He wanted it to happen and would let us know if Dawn felt well enough to attend.

Dawn did come down in her wheelchair to the dining room where well over a hundred people had gathered to celebrate and sing. Of course, she cried, which made her breathing more difficult, but she managed to say what a privilege it had been for her to live and serve in the community for so long. A special gluten-free chocolate cake was made for her. Curt stopped me later to say how much Dawn appreciated the celebration. She died four months later, on March 27, 2014, while resting in her room with Curt as they worked on their latest piece of poetry together. Curt survived Dawn by two years and died on a park bench two blocks from our house after taking a walk by Lake Michigan.

Dawn's passing marked a significant change in the

leadership of the community. For decades our pastoral team had consisted of eight people, four of whom were related to Dawn by either blood or marriage. Because of this, there were occasional accusations of nepotism, but I never saw any unhealthy or unfair advantages coming from these familial connections. We all lived and breathed the same lifestyle, with no one living in a condo on Lake Shore Drive. When the community hit difficult times, I believe their flesh and blood bond of family was a strength, not a weakness.

With Dawn no longer with us, I was asked by the other members of the pastoral team to reimagine some structural changes for the community, especially in regards to the leadership. After much prayerful consideration and counsel with others, we decided to add new people to the leadership group, eventually agreeing to add twice as many people as we had initially thought: four instead of two.

Changes in the community always came about slowly. Just prior to these leadership changes, we had to address changes in our antiquated system of cleaning our house. Because of our size, our household needs would be considered "industrial level" and the responsibilities for much of the work fell to the men. One long-term member, actually the wife of one of the pastors, was fond of saying, "I live here because the men do the dishes."

In a kitchen meeting one day, a young man named Tim who tended to have an obsessive-compulsiveness when it came to cleaning the house—a trait that was greatly appreciated and needed—said rather off-handedly, "Why don't we all clean the house?"

I said, "Hold that thought," and into the dark night I

went.

I came back with a complete overhaul, assigning men and women to groups with around thirty people in each. Care was given to assign each group an equal number of young and able-bodied people with those who had to do less. The jobs were no longer gender-specific as they had been for nearly forty years. Each group could dole out responsibilities as they saw fit. The responsibilities included answering phones and manning the front door, doing dishes, cleaning the kitchen, and mopping the dining room, as well as all other common areas on the first floor. It was a group's responsibility for an entire week, while everyone else was off. Each group would then be free for the next five weeks while a different group fulfilled the tasks.

I sent an email informing everyone of the forthcoming changes and proceeded to leave town to visit my family in Florida. By the time I landed in Florida, complaints about the proposed changes were pouring into my email box. Within a few short hours, I was inundated with what felt like "hate mail" from some in the community.

I returned after the long weekend to what had turned into a bit of a hornet's nest. I was accosted one evening by someone who lived on my floor who accused me of ruining her family's lives. She was upset that she and her husband had to spend thirty minutes cleaning up after dinner, which was valuable time away from her kids, who were ten and twelve years old. I suggested to her that she simply take turns with her husband.

At the time, it felt like the community might end due to this change. Who knew it wouldn't be theological concerns but people's attachment to their routines and comforts that could derail us? The outcry seemed to be, "But we've never done things that way before."

It took two months before the new regiment began. After the first week, the guy from our pest control company came to do his monthly spraying. He immediately noticed the difference and said, "Wow. What happened? Who's been cleaning the house?" Not only was the building finally being properly cleaned, but we were also actually enjoying a new spirit of camaraderie with each other. The woman who had angrily said I was destroying her family caught me in the dining room after a few weeks and said, "To the degree that I was upset with you, I'd like to match by saying thank you. The house is looking so much better, and even my kids love being a part of the clean-up crew."

This restructuring with the "clean teams" illustrated to me, again, how fragile life in a community can be and how seemingly trivial concerns can feel insurmountable. Thankfully, this one "unfixable" became somewhat fixed. The week before we initiated the change we had a community meeting where, as a joke, I was chased onto the stage while people shot nerf arrows at me. We all had a good laugh, which is vital for life in community. I, of course, had no idea that in less than three years I would come under a far more serious attack by arrows that were not nerf.

– Chapter Twenty-Seven –
An Unexpected Voicemail

It was snowing in Chicago, and I'd just finished swimming a mile at the Gill Park indoor pool. I was dressing to leave when I noticed a text from my brother saying to call as soon as possible. I felt a flash of dread. I'd been thinking that one day I would get a call about my dad passing away. But when Mark answered, he said, "Jan has taken her life."

I must have answered Mark or offered some acknowledgment that I heard what he said, but, in my shock, I only remember stumbling into a taxi, forgoing my usual coffee at Starbucks. After pulling up to the house, I quickly made my way to my room with all my emotions caught in my throat.

I had called Jan a couple of weeks earlier, but she hadn't picked up. When she called back, just days later, I wasn't free to take her call. I couldn't stop thinking about that missed call. What would Jan have said? What could I have done? But no. I knew my sister enough to realize that nothing I might have said would have helped. Jan was never one to allow any editorial privileges about her decisions.

I tried to reach Pegge, Mindy, and Kirsten but none of them picked up. I wanted them to have the news as soon as possible so I texted them. Mindy was the first to call. At the sound of her voice, my emotions became unbottled.

I thought back to the last time I'd seen my sister, five months earlier. Jan's husband, Wayne, was on a trip to visit some national parks with their special needs daughter, Jenna. Jan and I had a rare opportunity to spend time together, which we hadn't done since growing up in the same household some forty years earlier. During my week-long stay, we ate breakfast together every morning and shared our plans for the day. Mine consisted mostly of running errands, going to Starbucks, and visiting our dad. We'd meet up again for dinner and take in a movie. Jan loved going to see all the newly-released films. Occasionally, we'd dine out with our brother Mark and his wife, Ginny.

It was during that visit Jan told me she'd had a double mastectomy due to breast cancer. She hadn't told anyone at the time, which was just like her. In time, she was declared cancer-free, but due to her alcoholism, her liver was becoming impaired. In spite of the doctor's warning, her drinking continued to be a problem.

One morning, we ended up on the topic of suicide. We talked about the traditional view we'd learned as children that those who committed suicide went straight to hell. Jan wanted to know if I believed this. I told her that I didn't, saying that there are so many issues surrounding such a decision and that it is beyond our grasp and judgment. I added what I believe to be true, that God is merciful. Before the conversation concluded, Jan let me know that she would never let herself end up like our dad in a nursing home. I didn't think much about it at the time.

Jan was an athlete, a marathon runner, a tennis player, and could have been a professional golfer with her natural swing. She was faithful to her church, and at all church functions she could be found in the kitchen washing pots and pans.

Jan was meticulous to a fault. Every drawer and cabinet in her home was completely organized. Her photo albums were labeled and sorted by dates and categories. On the day she ended her life, she'd already written out a check to be mailed to our dad's assisted living place for the next month and had placed notes on every door for her husband telling him where her body would be, warning him not to let their daughter Jenna find her. Her memorial service at the San Jose Methodist Church was packed. Everyone loved Jan.

She had never loved herself.

When Kirsten got the news about her Aunt Jan, she was shaken. The similarities between the two of them were hard to ignore.

"That easily could have been me," Kirsten told me. By this time, she was three years sober and had begun to live out her moral inventory, owning the destructive path she'd been on.

I had learned a few things about myself, as well. I had taken the Enneagram Personality Test years before and learned that, as a number four, I am hard-wired to quickly sort through difficult emotional experiences to discover the silver lining. It's a trait that, some might argue, can give the impression that I am unfeeling. On the positive side, it allowed me to quickly shift my focus to being grateful for the rare opportunity Jan and I had to spend that week with each other.

Another positive aspect of my type is that I'm not one to dwell on "what ifs" or "what might have been." Yet, when I heard Kirsten say those words—that what happened to Jan could have happened to her—the countless hours I'd spent worrying about my daughter came rushing back.

With tears still falling, I told her, "I lived in fear for so long that this would be your end."

– Chapter Twenty-Eight –
Allegations Arise

The French writer Antoine Revarol said, "Familiarity is the root of the closest friendships as well as the intensest hatreds." A community such as ours naturally attracted broken people. Many with tragic or difficult pasts. Central to our shared life together was our mission of welcoming others.

As the community grew, so did the responsibilities regarding who we could welcome and who we could not. Sometimes the decision had to be referred to the entire pastoral board, especially if it was a family with children wanting to move in. Recognizing the community's limitations of who we could welcome was something we learned only from having boots on the ground. It wasn't something that could be gleaned from a book or a classroom setting. We were an island of misfits, which may have led people to think that we wanted to recruit or convert everyone to our way of life, but that wasn't the case. An intentional community such as ours is not for everyone. Jean Vanier said, "Some people are too rich in heart." When I first read that, I thought he was saying some people are just too selfish. But with time and experience, I began to understand that some are not helped by living in a crowded, oftentimes chaotic, high-energy environment. We were inner-city missionaries living with the pulse of the city and its restlessness. We weren't a cloistered community in a remote area surrounded by beautiful nature that allowed for extended periods of silence and meditation. Your moments of meditation might be found while standing in a dinner line, with no guarantee that others would not disturb you with questions. But for some, this environment, rather than one of quiet and solitude, was the road to healing and wholeness.

Once, I was giving a 'talk & tour' to a group of pastors entering our denomination. The Covenant Church was fond of using our community to demonstrate the diversity of its member churches. After a Q&A, a woman raised her hand and confessed, "I don't think I could do this."

I laughed and said, "Well, guess what? You don't have to!" While I believe everyone needs community, for some that need will be satisfied by having a few close friends to share openly with from time to time.

Throughout my forty-five years at Jesus People, it was not uncommon for people to show up unannounced. I was one of them. With that as my own experience, I never wanted to shut the door to the possibility that God would bring someone to our community not only for themselves but for us. After interviews, background and reference checks, only time would ultimately tell if it was going to work long term for the person or not. Nothing was more painful for me than the realization that some people could not be welcomed. How could I share the message of Christ's unconditional love to those who felt broken and unloved and then turn around and tell them they had to leave? It was the worst part of my job, and I didn't take it lightly. In Jean Vanier's book, *Community and Growth*, there is a section called "Sending People Away." It was this section that I reread most often. Vanier's approach to this aspect of a community's life was insightful and compassionate. He said the only rule with this matter is patience.

Occasionally, children who had grown up in the community left on bad terms. Some came to resent the unconventional lifestyle imposed on them by their parents. Unfortunately, for some, it was easier for them to direct that ill-will toward the community rather than toward their own parents.

Such seemed the case when a former member released a documentary in 2014 that reflected his own childhood with the Jesus People. In it, he alleged that the community was a breeding ground for child molestation practices. The filmmaker had lived with the Jesus People thirty years prior. He had been a particularly troubled boy. Due to his disturbing behavior, we had arranged to have him privately tutored while still making every effort to give him a sense of inclusion with his peers.

The documentary he released contained interviews with other former children raised in the community. The group alleged that all the children in the community had been fair game to the adult men. Of course, such a charge would include their own fathers as child molesters. One of the accusers had lived in foster homes before coming to be with us and had made the same claims against the men in her previous placements.

The Catholic Church sex abuse scandal had broken in 2002 and, in the thirteen years since, allegations of this type were surfacing regularly in the news. Sexual abuse was being revealed in countless organizations, from the Boy Scouts to synagogues and public schools. By the end of 2015, the feature film "Spotlight" would dramatize more than fifteen years of sex abuse among Catholic priests. No area of society was immune from these stories; still, I was heartbroken to see our community come under fire as well.

Yet I was equally discouraged to discover that the truth seemed unimportant. I would never dismiss the severity of sexual abuse, especially with children. Since our earliest days as a community, whenever there were suspicions that someone was crossing boundaries, those matters were immediately addressed, especially if they involved children. In retrospect, we should have asked the documentarian's family to move out for the welfare of their son, but the community was young and inexperienced at that time. Instead, a couple of our pastors, school counselors, and nearby neighbors worked closely with his parents to find solutions. The family finally moved out when he was an older teenager. After graduating from high school, he asked to come back to be part of our magazine's art staff while he finished his education at the Art Institute of Chicago.

Though I considered the documentary to be largely based on sensationalism, I was surprised that so many supposed friends who had known our community for years just accepted the claims as valid. The very mention of child molestation is like going for the jugular. It's the bell that can't be unrung. As pastors, we weren't free to argue or discuss the charges publicly. There was a degree of confidentiality that had to be respected because the accusers had been in our congregation. When a former community member and golfing buddy of mine sent me a message saying, "I watched the documentary and believe it all to be the truth. What do you have to say?" I wrote back, "Nothing, since your mind is already made up."

Sadly, I never got the sense that the participants in the documentary were seeking healing. They never named their abusers, yet they made these claims against not only our community, but the Evangelical Covenant Church as well, even though Jesus People USA was not affiliated with the ECC at the time of the alleged abuses. I was asked by the pastoral board to aid the attorneys who were representing us during the discovery process. As a result, I was aware that, at one point, the documentarian contacted the superintendent of the Central Conference, Rev. Jerome Nelson. The conversation between the two became rather charged and Rev. Nelson asked, "Are you saying that the pastors of Jesus People molested children in the community? If so, I have lawyers on speed dial to contact for matters like that."

The documentarian replied, "No. I'm not saying that."

An official lawsuit was never filed. The documentarian, who was initially one of the group of claimants, was dropped by his attorneys because of his lack of cooperation. He refused to be confidential, taking any and all interviews that came his way. Nevertheless, agreements were made to move forward with what is referred to as a "discovery period." My role was to work with our in-house attorney and outside representing counsel to conduct interviews to see if we could find any corroboration with any of the claims.

The allegations caused great harm to the community, and it proved to be a tenuous, difficult path forward. The community survived it by continuing to do the good works that we were committed to. I reminded myself that Jesus was called the son of Beelzebub and that didn't stop his acts of mercy and kindness. We tried to follow this example by keeping an open heart and open door in spite of the suspicions that had been raised and made public.

It wasn't until later that I would look back and believe a seed had been planted during the conversation between the documentarian and the superintendent. In order for the claimants to include the deeper pocket of the ECC, they would have to name someone who was not simply part of the leadership team, but a pastor ordained by the Evangelical Covenant Church.

Someone like me.

– Chapter Twenty-Nine –
A Charge is Made

The discovery period we entered into with the claimants stretched from the average six months to a year and then another. In January 2017, during one of the weekly visits with our representing attorney, he pulled me aside and said, "I hate to tell you this, but now a claim has been made against you."

When I heard the name of my accuser, I recalled that this same person had posted allegations against me on Facebook six or seven years earlier. I had shared the posting with the other pastors, deleted the post, blocked him from my Facebook account, and moved on.

This person wasn't a stranger to me. He was the younger son of the woman who came to find support from our community in the late seventies. Pegge and I had cared for all three of her children while she grappled with finding stability for herself. We had done our best to provide a stable environment for her children while they were with us. Revoral's quote about familiarity being the root of the "intensest hatreds" came to me. How had I become the enemy?

Shortly thereafter, I attended the Midwinter Conference annual pastors gathering in Louisville, Kentucky. I intentionally sought out the executive minister, Rev. Mark

Novak, along with his associate, Rev. Carol Lawson, to inform them of the allegations made against me. They listened to the story, prayed for me, and told me to consider myself under the care of the Board of the Ordered Ministry, the licensing and caring board for ECC pastors.

I was greatly relieved to share with them and receive their prayers and support. When I got back to Chicago, naturally I shared with the other leaders about my conversation, and life moved forward as usual. I was serving my second year as part of the Commission on Ministerial Standing (COMS), which is a board that initiates licensure and ordination with the Covenant Church. We met twice each year to read the ordination papers from the candidates and conduct in-person interviews. The new leaders added to our pastoral board were part of those interviewed to receive bi-vocational licenses. That license required each of them to have an ordained minister as their mentor. I filled that role for all of them. I also chaired the Central Conference board of spiritual directors.

Life could not have been more full. Our community had been engaged in creative measures to reach our Uptown neighbors, a diverse group that was rapidly changing due to gentrification. Church attendance within our own community had been dwindling, so we engaged in an out-of-the-box restructure by doing a church plant in our own community's church service. The hope was to become a place where others did not feel they were simply visiting the church of Jesus People USA, but one they could call their home church, too.

We began an elongated process of discernment with pastors and professors at the North Park Seminary. After six months of discussion and clarifying our intentions, we identified a person who was willing to consider the challenge of becoming the pastor with this new initiative. After a few months, she said, "There are nine things out of ten that are all positive for me, but there is one thing that keeps me from accepting. I don't feel called." Not sensing a call overrides all the positives. It was disappointing, but it did not keep us from moving forward.

Surprisingly, a few months into the process, a person graduating from the seminary heard about our venture and sought me out to learn more. He didn't know anything about the previous candidate, but after praying with his wife, he said, "I wanted to let you know that my wife and I are feeling called to do this with you, if you will have us." He became central to the project with the new church plant.

In May 2017, I was able to visit my longtime friend and mentor, Jean Vanier, at his community in France. We shared meals and had daily conversations about life in our communities. He was already experiencing some difficulties walking through his little village, so he would lean on my shoulder during our walks.

I told him about the allegations made against me, and let him know that I was contemplating stepping out of my leadership role. Jean surprised me by suggesting that I take a year-long sabbatical, which I found disturbing. It was not customary for our community. "There is life after leadership," he said. This was something I'd never taken time to imagine.

Then, on one of our walks, Jean stopped, looked at me, and said, "Neil, you are a true follower of Jesus." I was greatly honored to hear such words from a man I deeply respected. His words could not have meant more to me if they had come from St. Peter himself.

After my visit with Jean, I arrived home in June. I shared with my pastoral team the delight of my trip and the exchanges I had with Jean.

Less than a week later, while sitting at my desk preparing for the Sunday service, I received a phone call from the executive minister of the Board of the Ordered Ministry, Rev. Mark Novak. He said that he had been told he had to suspend my license as a Covenant pastor, and let me know that he had cried when he got the news. At the time I had no idea what suspension meant, but I would quickly find out the following day. Suspension meant that I could no longer preach or teach in any Covenant church, and I could no longer attend our own church service. Just the month before, I had spoken at the morning chapel service to the seminarians and faculty at the North Park Theological Seminary. Weeks before that, I had sat with the COMS Board to approve others' licensure and/or ordination. In fact, I was asked to moderate an interview with someone who had questionable issues. I was fully engaged with our new church plant initiative. Another Covenant spiritual director and I had just spent four days offering spiritual direction to new pastors moving into our denomination from other affiliations.

Rev. Novak informed me that I needed to attend the ECC annual meeting being held that month in Detroit, Michigan to meet with the Board of the Ordered Ministry. I was told to bring one support person. I chose my friend, Rev. Jay Phelan, the president of the North Park Seminary. Jay had been a long-time advocate of our community since we joined the ECC in 1989. He and I had been meeting together for lunch once a month for six or seven years. Jay was intimately acquainted with the Board of the Ordered Ministry, having been a member of it for fourteen years.

We arrived a half hour before the meeting began. We saw many familiar faces, many offering encouraging words. The superintendent, Rev. Jerome Nelson, attended another meeting, saying it was far more serious than mine.

The meeting began with introductions, then I was asked to share the circumstances of what brought me there. Our community was well-known throughout the Covenant, but I thought a review of our ministries would be helpful and put things in context. I shared how our community welcomed people who are oftentimes in distress and need support in ways that a typical church can't offer. I shared how Pegge and I, as a young couple, had been asked to support a woman who had come to our community hoping to regain stability in her life, and that Pegge and I had made every effort to provide a loving family environment for the children, helping them with their school work and including them in family outings and vacations. And how now, thirty-five years later, my wife and I were being accused of abusing the youngest boy, even though throughout our forty-plus years in the community there had never been any concerns raised about our behavior with children. I told them about the documentary and the group of claimants who purported that the children in our community were like "candy" for all the adult men, which would, of course, implicate their own fathers. I pointed out that the allegation against me came only after the documentarian had had a conversation with the conference superintendent, where I believe he realized the importance of accusing an ordained minister with the ECC. When I concluded my story, a question and answer period followed. I was asked how I prayed for my accuser. I answered by quoting Henri Nouwen, who said, "To pray is to open your hands."

"So that is what I do," I said. "I sit with God in silence with my hands open, offering myself, offering this situation with my denomination and offering those who raised false allegations against me, my wife, and our community." I concluded by saying, "I know what it is like to live life dishonestly before God, and it is a terrible, lonely existence."

Then Jay and I were asked to leave the room. A half hour later we were called back in. A letter of resolution from the board was read aloud. It stated that my suspension was being upheld and that I was to return the following year to meet with the board again. I was asked to attend a counseling clinic for my own personal growth, which would be funded by the ECC.

Jay spoke up. He said he found this to be unbelievable and could not fathom why they were upholding the suspension. On the way out, he had an exchange with the acting executive minister, Rev. Dick Lucco, and let him know in unequivocal, colorful terms that this was a bullshit decision.

Later, on the ride back to Chicago, I told Jay, "Thank you for expressing what I was not free to say."

– Chapter Thirty –
Stepping Down

I returned to the community and assumed my normal routine of attending leadership meetings, giving counsel to those in need, and dealing with the unexpected problems others brought my way. We continued to move forward with the hopes of creating and expanding our church service beyond our own membership.

The team of pastors in my community, with its newly-added members, told me they wanted to have some part of the weekly meetings without me present. I didn't think much about it since I'd already expressed my desire to step off the leadership team when the time seemed appropriate. I assumed we would all come to an agreement over how that would be done.

After the Board of the Ordered Ministry issued their letter of resolution upholding my suspension, I took it upon myself to write a letter of disagreement with their decision and emailed it to those on my leadership team, thinking we would all want to sign it. The letter was never mentioned at the next meeting, so I emailed it again to everyone. I also sent the letter to our attorney who was representing the community against the abuse claims. He told me he was impressed with the letter and that he, too, was caught off guard by the denomination suspending my license. In fact, he wondered if something had happened recently that led them to their decision, now, five months later.

The following week at our Monday morning coffee gathering, in an unexpected turnabout, our own in-house legal counsel, along with the other members of the pastoral board, presented a letter to be read to me. It stipulated that I was not to have any contact or involvement with minors and outlined certain boundaries about where I would be allowed to go throughout the house and our other buildings. The team assured me it wasn't that they believed the allegations against me, but they were trying to show that they too were handling things responsibly. The consensus was that they needed to protect themselves in the same way the ECC was protecting itself.

After the letter was read aloud, I paused for a moment, and then said, "I would never sign such a document." I pointed out that the document did not address the fact that Pegge and I lived right next door to two minor children, the granddaughters of one of the pastors I'd served with for over forty years. And I argued that if there was a legitimate concern on everyone's part for the children's welfare in our house, then I should be asked to leave.

Some were genuinely surprised at my resistance to the letter. I honestly believe they felt they were doing the right thing. The following week, the document was amended, granting me permission to see my grandson should my daughter Kirsten visit from Omaha. Then our in-house attorney, in the presence of my other co-pastors, said, "Either sign the document or leave."

Leaving the community was something neither Pegge or I had ever entertained. In forty-three years of marriage, we had never once had a conversation about leaving the place we had both felt called to as young single people. I believe this action actually brought about a psychological crisis of denial for my wife. It is common knowledge amongst clergy that spouses often suffer more in situations like these. The following week, I told the leadership team that Pegge and I were going to leave for a year-long sabbatical.

A community-wide communication was sent out saying: "Important meeting. Please attend or have a family member attend." My daughter, Mindy, who lived in Chicago, attended. When it came time for me to speak, I was overwhelmed with emotion and cried for almost five minutes. I announced I was stepping down from my role as a leader in the community after forty-three years and that Pegge and I felt it was best for us to leave for a year to allow everyone to step into their leadership roles without me being present. I did not mention the document I refused to sign. I was unwilling to become the person causing a division in the community I had loved and labored with for so many years. It was unimaginable for me to think about where it all might lead. *Who's for Neil? Who isn't?* The pain of this was already more than I'd ever imagined, and engaging in a battle that I might lose would have only exacerbated it.

Mindy, who knew all the details, cried the whole way through the meeting. Afterwards, a childhood friend of hers who was now a member of the leadership team said, "I don't know why your dad wouldn't just sign the document."

Mindy shot back at her, saying, "I can promise you, I would have never asked your mother, who I have known all my life, to sign such a thing."

There were times when my wife and daughters were confounded by my determination to look forward, not backward. As a Type Four on the Enneagram, one of my key strengths is equanimity. I am quick to find good in bad situations. Perhaps with this strength of equanimity may come a potential to sidestep dealing with grief and pain. I had always appreciated being in community because I learned much from observing the response others had that I may have been oblivious to in my quest for equanimity. In this case, my family worried that I wasn't reacting enough. In some ways it was a kind of deja vu experience for me. When I joined the community forty-five years earlier, I was completely clear about my sense of calling to move into the community, and now I was equally as clear about leaving. I knew action steps had to be taken, and the emotional whiplash would have to be dealt with after.

Before leaving the Chicago area, I attended the counseling center the ECC had recommended and funded. It was a three-day-long evaluation using many standard testing tools, including a psychiatric evaluation. In mid-September, after Pegge and I had already moved out, only the Board of the Ordered Ministry and I received a copy of the assessment from the Midwest Ministry Development Center. It read:

> Based on a three-day program of vocational and psychological assessment and counseling, Mr. Taylor has been seen as a person of sound character and as an effective and spiritually-rooted pastor leader by the community at JPUSA and the ECC. Nothing from the assessment process suggests otherwise. His trust

that God is at work in his life and the life of the community seems genuine and not defensive or self-deluding.

– Chapter Thirty-One –
Living in Exile

Suddenly, it was time to go. I was grateful to Jean Vanier for suggesting a one-year sabbatical and knew it was the right decision.

Pegge and I asked Kirsten to find us an apartment near her in Omaha. Like Mindy, Kirsten was in shock about what was happening, but on the other hand, the prospect of us moving to Omaha was like a dream come true for her. It was something she thought would never happen in a thousand years, and I would have agreed with her.

In our entire married lives, Pegge and I had never had many choices about our living space. Now, we were able to make some requests. Pegge wanted a balcony, and I wanted to be on the first floor. Those two things are typically incompatible. One day, Kirsten was being shown a number of apartments in a nice complex but none seemed suitable. Finally, the manager said, "I have one more apartment I can show you." She led her to the back of one of the buildings to an apartment that was on the first floor but, because there was a basement apartment below, it also had a balcony that overlooked a forest preserve. Kirsten made the down payment that very day. Leaving our community had been the farthest thing from our minds, but we began again in a new place, near our daughter, her husband, and our grandson in a two-bedroom apartment on the first floor with a balcony.

Three friends from the community, Dave, Teel, and Andrew, helped us move some of our belongings and made the drive with us. Our room in Chicago was left intact for the year we'd be gone. When we arrived in Omaha, Kirsten met us at the door and showed us furniture she'd gathered from Craigslist and Nextdoor. After moving everything in, we talked about going to dinner together, but I told them to go ahead without us, saying, "I think I prefer to stay and start getting settled in."

Teel jokingly said, "This is feeling like an 'Old Yeller' moment."

I managed to chuckle. Pegge and I walked them to their vehicle. We thanked them and hugged everyone good-bye, then I quickly turned away, afraid they'd see the tears pouring from my eyes.

It's hard to know where to start after living most of your adult life with three to four hundred people every day, then finding yourself in an apartment complex where you don't know anyone. Pegge and I are both friendly people, but sometimes friendliness puts other people off. Not long after, we met our next door neighbors. They had two young boys, and when my daughter came over with our grandson, they would play in the hallway together. That felt familiar. The hallways of the large Chelsea hotel that housed the community in Chicago had always been filled with ball-playing, tricycles, and doll houses.

Our building was supposed to be a non-smoking building, but there was a constant smell of skunk weed coming from one of the apartments nearby. We weren't the only ones to complain about it. The manager even queried my wife about how she used to deal with these matters in the low-income housing unit she had managed for twenty years. Then, one of the maintenance guys reported to the manager that he believed the marijuana smell was coming from our apartment. By our second week, we received a notice of eviction that claimed we had violated the smoking ban.

Kirsten was over that day, and we showed her the notice. She immediately went over to have it out with the manager. The young woman tried to downplay it, saying that the complaint would disappear from our rental history after six months. I wrote to the corporate office explaining the situation, and the manager was replaced within the week. In our first year there, the manager changed three times, though not because of us. My daughter wanted us to move out immediately, but Pegge and I liked our apartment and its amenities. It was the most room we'd ever had in forty-three years of marriage!

After a month or two of living in our apartment, we became friendly with a couple who lived directly above us on the second floor. They had a baby girl. Our one-and-a-half-year-old grandson Max enjoyed climbing the stairs while we chased him. One day Max went up the stairs and opened the door to what he thought was our apartment. The young mother heard me yelling for Max and she called out, "Max, is that you? Have you come to visit us?"

I apologized profusely for Max bursting in. Max tried to do the same thing a couple of weeks later; fortunately, this time their door was locked. When Max wouldn't go back downstairs with me, I grabbed the door handle and jiggled it to show him that it was locked because it was not our apartment.

The next week, I was coming into the apartment complex and greeted the young dad, saying, "Hey Daniel. How are you? I haven't seen y'all around lately."

Daniel said he'd been sick and was staying inside.

I said I was sorry to hear it.

He replied, "I don't want you to greet us or speak to me or my family anymore. I read about your community and watched the documentary. I don't care if these are just allegations or not, I'd just appreciate you staying away. Plus, I was on the inside of our apartment when you tried to get in."

This wasn't a conversation, so I simply said, "Done."

There are no words to properly explain the pain of being castigated as a child molester after having served faithfully in a community as a pastor for over forty years. Or the shock of seeing an internet article that read, "The Evangelical Covenant church upholds suspension of Pastor Neil Taylor for allegations of child molestation" with a photo of me holding my grandson in my arms.

I had attempted to share with my own leadership team the mental fatigue that comes from being accused by such an allegation. I suffered wondering what others were thinking of me and found myself becoming introspective about every conversation and every interaction, even just smiling at a child.

I spent countless hours replaying the events that had led to this point.

Now that Pegge and I had left, I began the process of unpacking all the pent-up emotions and feelings I had to ignore while giving care to my family and community. I now felt deeply embarrassed that I had written a letter in defense of myself expecting that the leadership team would sign it and send it to the denomination. At the time, I felt it was a letter any one of us on the leadership team would have sent to the denomination on behalf of any one of us. I was clueless that everyone else was on another track and that they were writing up a document limiting not only my movement in the community, but also my participation in ministry.

I told myself that the decisions others made were ones I would have never made, especially regarding people I knew were innocent. I believe I would 'go down with the ship' for an innocent person. It was hard for me to imagine choosing self-protection from legal liabilities over standing with the falsely-accused.

As I sat alone in my apartment, other sentences came back to haunt me: "We're trying to find a way to keep you from having to leave," one person offered. And after my announcement that Pegge and I were leaving for a year, a new person on the leadership team told me, "Now we can be friends again."

In time, Pegge and I formed new connections. I knew some of the pastors in the Evangelical Covenant churches in Omaha, so we visited them on Sundays. One was particularly close in proximity, so we began attending each week. I knew the wife of the co-pastor team, Dawn Burnett, who was a trained spiritual director like myself. We had been involved in joint gatherings of spiritual directors at some of the Covenant's annual meetings. She and her husband Andrew, known as Roo, were ordained in 2004, the same year I was. The two of them were extremely gracious and welcoming to us. They were thrilled to have a pastor from Jesus People as part of their congregation, and I was invited to attend their weekly staff and vision team meetings.

After what had happened with my neighbor Daniel, it dawned on me that the same thing could happen at their church. I went to visit Roo and told him that Pegge and I would not be coming to the church any longer, fearing our presence could get them into trouble with members of their congregation. I believed it would be better for them if we attended a church where we would be anonymous. Roo said he believed that he and Dawn could handle it if anything ever came up.

I told him I felt like Sigourney Weaver's character, Ripley, in the movie *Aliens*, and said, "Roo, I have seen the alien. You haven't."

Soon after, Roo's wife Dawn called and said, "I heard about your decision to no longer come to church with us. But I want to say, I like a good sequel." I knew what she meant. In *Aliens*, the sequel to the first movie *Alien*, Ripley goes back to face the aliens.

I said, "We don't really want to leave, but in order to stay I feel it is only right for me to share my story with the Board of Elders at the church."

At the next meeting, the board listened to my account of how I ended up in Omaha and the ordeal I'd gone through with the ECC and my own community. I will never forget the candid response from one of the board members, Paul, who said, "Why in the hell would you ever have anything to do with a Covenant church?"

Pastor Andrew answered for me and said, "It is family."

We still attend the church, where I help lead Bible studies and preach occasionally. I was also able to continue receiving and giving spiritual direction in our new home.

I received a suggestion to contact Father Lorn Snow at the St. John's Cathedral on the campus of Creighton University. I wrote to him, explaining who I was and my experience with spiritual direction. We began meeting monthly, the typical rhythm for spiritual direction. His intentional listening provided much necessary support, especially in those early, dark, lonely days.

My son-in-law Tyler, an avowed atheist, gave me a book for Christmas that year. It was *The Book Of Joy* by the Dalai Lama and Archbishop Desmond Tutu.

In it, the archbishop said to his friend, the Dalai Lama, "Many people look at you and they think of all the awful things that have happened to you. Nothing can be more devastating than being exiled from your home, from the things that are really precious to you. And yet when people come to you, they experience someone who has a wonderful serenity . . . a wonderful compassion . . . a mischievousness . . ."

This helped me identify a pain I truly feel. I am in exile. I can only hope that my own sense of compassion and mischievousness will not only remain intact, but might flourish and grow. Someone once told me that for every ten years of devotion to something, it takes one year of distancing in order to heal.

If that is true, I would need four and a half years to heal.

– Chapter Thirty-Two –
Three Things

In Spring 2018, I received a voicemail one evening from Rev. Theresa Marks informing me that the ECC was interested in lifting my suspension. She had a sense of excitement in her voice, but for me, excitement had become a foreign emotion. The damage done was irreversible. I called back the following day to discover that the board wanted my permission to contact my accuser.

More than a year had passed. I said, "Wow. First of all, I'm shocked to discover you need my permission. I would think this would have been the first thing this office would have done on behalf of one of its clergy, whether you have permission or not. But yes, you have my permission."

In June that year, Pegge and I traveled to Minneapolis to the Covenant's annual meeting for our scheduled return appointment with the Board of the Ordered Ministry. This time, since Pegge was coming with me, we both took a support person. When we arrived at the conference center, we were surprised to discover that some members of the leadership team from Jesus People had driven all night to show support for me. They weren't invited to be in the meeting and waited in the lounge area.

Jay Phelan went with me again and my long-time friend and former co-pastor, Tom Cameron, went as

Pegge's support person. Knowing I was going to be asked how my year had been, I'd prepared a four-page response, believing it would be difficult to give an answer extemporaneously.

I began by sharing how grateful I had been when Jesus People became a member church with the ECC in 1989. I found many companions in the ECC and, because of this, it was difficult for me to express the disappointment with my experience.

When I contacted the ECC in January 2017 to self-report the charges, I naively believed that I would receive help from the denomination I had served for many years. The board had never received a complaint about me from an outside source. I had personally informed the leadership about the abuse allegations made against me. Five months passed before they decided to take what felt to me like a "duck and cover" approach by suspending my license and leaving me to survive on my own.

I reminded the group that, in the past, any and all allegations against our community had been investigated responsibly by the ECC. In the early 90s, Jesus People USA had been included in a book on abusive churches by an author who was eventually criticized by his own sociology contemporaries for his blatant lack of ethical methodology. Ten years later, an article in the Chicago Tribune put the community under a microscope because some members chose to leave, revealing nothing more than a matter resembling a church split—something many congregations experience. Finally, we found ourselves the target of a more insidious attack alleging the Jesus People to be like the Catholic Church, deliberately covering for sex offenders and exposing children to further harm.

"It's been my observation that these claimants aggressively enlist whoever they can to make accusations in order to lend credence to their claims," I said. "But with a little investigation it would have been easy to discover a connection with former disgruntled members who have attacked our community over the years, dating back to when we first became a member church of the ECC."

I went on to say, "I am in support of suspension over agreed standards set for the clergy of the ECC, but not without due process. I believe with a little effort, surely in the five months prior to my suspension, it could have been discovered that complaints of this nature have never previously been raised about me or my wife during our forty-five year history at Jesus People, where we both joined as teenagers."

I told the board that my life would never be the same. My year-long sabbatical had been more like a year spent riding out a storm. The questions I now lived with and faced daily were: Where to from here? And what would it look like if I was truly forgiving not only to my accusers, but my own church family as well?

I closed by saying, "I am asking that this board, along with the leadership of the ECC, do its investigation into allegations made towards its clergy. Obviously, some matters require immediate attention and action, but the idea of a Zero Tolerance Policy that advocates action before investigation is basically communicating guilty until proven innocent. This type of policy is highly criticized by many, including the American Psychological Association, citing its potential to be egregiously unfair, draconian, and ultimately providing little benefit. I now join ranks with these critics from my own experience of being acted against without due diligence and having suffered its consequences, in being uprooted and now having my reputation questioned."

I finished reading the letter, handed it to the chairperson, and sat down. The room was silent except for the sound of my wife quietly crying. Finally, the acting Executive Minister of the Board, Rev. Dick Lucco, with tears in his eyes, said, "We failed you in the way this was handled. All we can do is ask for forgiveness and we will make reparations."

Rev. Greg Applequist began the question-answer period by asking, "Do you have any idea where to go from here?"

All I could say was, "No, I don't. I cannot imagine not living in my community, nor can I imagine not living near my grandson."

A longtime pastor and friend to whom I'd given spiritual direction for two or three years said, "I am so sorry, Neil. You have been there for me so often, and now I realize I completely failed you by not being there for you. I never even called. Please forgive me."

Pegge and I, along with our two support people, Jay Phelan and Tom Cameron, left the meeting to give the board time to discuss the matter and write up their letter of resolution. When they were ready for us to return, I took my seat and listened as their resolution was read aloud:

June 27, 2018, from the Board of the Ordered Ministry:

We grieve the malicious accusations against Jesus People USA in general and you specifically. We receive your admonition of the lack of care and due process provided to you and to your family by the Board of the Ordered Ministry and the staff of Develop Leaders. We are deeply sorry, and we humbly receive your forgiveness.

We affirm your journey this past year in conversation with trusted friends, mentors, and spiritual directors. We affirm the discomfort of sitting with your frustration, disappointment, anger, and desire to receive and extend forgiveness. We are grateful for your life of gratitude and your conscious dependence on the risen Christ. We celebrate the deep connection that you and Pegge have with your daughter, son-in-law, and grandson. We also acknowledge, affirm, and celebrate your 45 years of faithful ministry.

The Committee lifts Neil's suspension and releases him from care of the Board. We pray that Neil would continue to journey well with Jesus.

Prayers were offered and the meeting ended. My wife went to Dick Lucco and asked if they could do something about the article on the internet. My support person, Jay, made his way to the waiting room to address those from the Jesus People leadership team who had traveled to offer support to me.

Rev. Theresa Marks stopped him and said, with a smile, "See, if you just trust the process..."

Jay said, "Hardly. The process is what got us here in the first place." Then he turned to those present from the Jesus People leadership team and said, "I want to make abundantly clear to you what just happened in there. They admitted to completely mishandling this with Neil, and, in my opinion, you have also."

The next morning, I had breakfast with President Emeritus Rev. Paul Larsen. When he heard the story, he advised me to get legal counsel. I chuckled. But he was serious.

I reminded him that the board had apologized and that my suspension had been lifted.

He said, "You don't just burn a man's house down and then say, 'Sorry.'"

Pegge and I drove back to Omaha later that day. I was told that Paul Larsen made the rounds to speak plainly to the various church officials about what they had done and about what the reparations should look like.

Later that week, I received a phone call from President Emeritus Rev. Glenn Palmberg. He said, "I seriously think you need to get legal counsel to handle the matter of reparations with the ECC."

My whole life has been about learning to listen to wise counsel and here were two past presidents of the denomination—men who often did not see eye to eye over many matters—telling me the same thing.

I turned to a Chicago attorney, Pat Reardon, who graduated seminary to become a priest with the Catholic Church and instead became an attorney. Pat and his partner, Mark Solock, were exactly who I needed to help navigate matters forward. I certainly had no experience with such things.

Pat Reardon and Mark Solock met with the ECC's legal counsel. Pat said the conversation began a bit tense but by the end the ECC's legal counsel agreed with them about compensation. He said he would speak to his clients and get back to them. Pat and Mark were never able to meet with him again. He was never in when they called and none of their correspondence was ever returned.

The ECC's apology was in word only.

President Emeritus Glenn Palmberg reached out on my behalf to the newly installed president of the denomination, Rev. John Wenrich. The response to Glenn was short and succinct, saying, "We are not in negotiation with Neil Taylor. The new executive minister for the Board of the Ordered Ministry, Rev. Lance Davis, and I are looking for a job for Neil. If you have ideas, please let us know."

I never received one phone call from the ECC about a job opportunity.

Pat Reardon, who was recently retired, was not willing to push forward with a lawsuit, yet he advised me to do so and said he would look for another attorney for me. He forwarded me a copy of the final correspondence he sent to the leaders of the ECC and their legal counsel:

My years before retirement taught me that both the running of a church and the practice of law place great demands on time and schedules. So I can be sympathetic to some delays. I am just an old guy who does not need to make judgments any more. Nevertheless, I must say that the delay and lack of attention or action to Rev. Taylor's concerns has begun to seem more than just the product of time constraints. Another entire year has passed since Neil's original year of extreme difficulty. In my many years of representing religious personnel I have never encountered the inattention that Neil Taylor is experiencing.

If my judgment is flawed and there is some sincerity for promptly dealing with this excellent minister's welfare, I am available at any time. Please communicate with me by telephone or email.

In the meantime, best wishes for personal peace in this Easter Season.

Pat Reardon

The newly installed executive minister contacted me to say that he wanted to redress my situation and urged me to trust him. Six months later, he called to let me know that nothing would be done for me by the ECC. I thanked him for telling me and knew I would have to move forward with a lawsuit. Before doing so, I sent out a message to the private Facebook page for ECC ministers. I wanted to inform the ministerium why I was compelled to take legal action. When I shared my situation with a friend whose daughter is now a licensed minister with the ECC, he responded, "Thank you. I'm glad to hear it because I would not want what happened to you to happen to her."

I did not want what happened to me to happen to any of the ministerium.

Whenever anyone asked me, "How are you doing with all of this?" my reply was, "I've already been to hell. There is no greater hell than living with the fear of losing your own child to a life of drugs."

I believe I was, in some way, prepared to face this ordeal because of what I had gone through with Kirsten's fifteen-year drug addiction. My training in spiritual direction was also invaluable, deepening my personal awareness of God's presence in all things, even through these horrific and difficult events. I became well-practiced in self-care and am blessed to have friends who regularly call or write to check up on me. Their support has been incredibly helpful as I live the life that I now face.

Ultimately, I became clear about the three things I wanted as reparations from the Covenant Church. The first consideration was monetary since what I had in place for retirement in my community was no longer there. Secondly, Rev. Davis had promised a public apology would be made to me in front of the ministerium. In spite of my objections, he was insistent that I attend an honorary dinner for ECC ministers who had given outstanding service, assuring me the apology would take place there. I specifically asked a few people to be present to witness this. There were many recognitions offered throughout the meal, but the dinner ended without any apology to me. When I asked Lance about it the next day, he said, "It wasn't the right time." Finally, I had asked that the Letter of Resolution from the board lifting my suspension be read to my community. He agreed to do it, but to my knowledge that has never happened either.

Before my year away from Jesus People came to an end, I received word that, in order to return to the community, I would need to undergo further psychological testing to determine whether I was a safe person. This would supposedly protect them if they encountered any legal issues in regard to me. This was something I knew I would not subject someone to when I knew their innocence. But I had stepped aside from my leadership role and had lost the ability to influence decisions for the community. This request became the tipping point for me to realize that Pegge and I would not return to living in the community.

I'd been committed to Jesus People USA practically from the start. There was little doubt in my mind about joining, and it was my life's work. Someone once said, "Your imprint is everywhere in the community."

When I heard those words, I remember praying, "God, please let that imprint be Yours, not mine."

– Chapter Thirty-Three –
When All is Said and Done

In September 2018, the pastors from Celebration Covenant Church in Omaha were going to be away on vacation and asked me to take the pulpit. Interestingly, that Sunday would mark exactly one year since I had left the community. The assigned text was from the gospel of John 15:1-17. Part of this well-known passage is often inscribed or etched into the lintels above the doorway in many churches: *I am the vine; you are the branches.* As I pondered the verses throughout this passage for the hundredth time, it struck me afresh that this part of the gospel contains the departing words of Christ to his disciples before his arrest and execution. John records them as being said just after the institution of the Lord's Supper and the washing of the disciple's feet. In a sense, these are like Jesus saying, "So before I die, I want to tell you..." He said, "This is my commandment, that you love another as I have loved you. No one has greater love than this, to lay down one's life for one's friends. You are my friends..."

When I thought of how Jesus claimed his disciples as friends, I closed the Bible and wept. I knew it was no accident that I was asked to preach on these verses. Friendship is and has always been my greatest longing. It was very difficult for me to craft the sermon that Sunday as I sat with the absence of so many of my longtime relationships. I identified with Jesus's longing for friendship, yet I knew full well how the story ends. His friends deny that they ever knew Him. There is a sense of comfort that comes in the discovery of being counted worthy to suffer in some small way as Christ did. Some may accuse me of having a Christ complex. But that is far from the truth. I've never saved or died for anyone.

Whenever I am tempted to dwell on my loss of friendships, I think of Dawn, my mentor and friend of nearly forty years. Before she passed away, she and her husband Curt wrote a poem for me as a birthday present. It is one of my most treasured gifts.

> *When all is said and done*
> *When the last lines have been drawn*
> *Enemies forgiven,*
> *Comrades in arms embraced.*
> *When the nations*
> *And the cities*
> *Are at best, co-belligerents,*
> *When it has come down to*
> *War and rumors of wars,*
> *Rampant revenge.*
> *When friendship has become rare*
> *Then, we know, He as well as you*
> *Will still be there.*

In the book *Stations of the Cross* by Timothy Radcliffe, he includes a quote from Gregory Roberts's *Shantaram*, "For this is what we do. Put one foot forward and then the other. Lift our eyes to the snarl and smile of the world once more... Drag our shadowed crosses into the hope of another night. Push our brave hearts into the promise of a new day... For so long as fate keeps us waiting, we live on."

I no longer live with the community that welcomed me, uninvited, in Gainesville, Florida back in the fall of 1972. I live in a two-bedroom apartment with two bathrooms, a luxury Pegge and I have never had. I have a view out my window of a forest preserve and often glance out to see as many as ten deer grazing and running by in the field. In the winter, I'm often delighted by the sight of a lone red cardinal alighted on a barren branch of a leafless tree. I believe God sees that bird and I trust that He sees me, too. I still swim three times a week at a local pool. Every lap is dedicated to prayer for relatives, friends, and my family and friends at Jesus People. Perhaps swimming laps is my rosary.

I talk to my daughters once or twice a day and live within a mile of my daughter Kirsten, who I had feared for years I would lose. My grandson, Max, and I swim together on Sunday afternoons and often go sledding after snowfalls. Someone said, "If you can retire with a grandchild nearby, it helps." There's something marvelously connecting for Max and me, despite our sixty-year spanse. In fact, as I write this, I am sitting at a golf course watching my grandson, Max, starting golf lessons with an organization called First Tee. It won't be long before he will be hitting the ball farther than his Pops and shooting a lower score than me. I look forward to enjoying that journey with him. I have finally arrived in life where I have a deep sense of no longer needing to win, which feels like a win to me.

Though I'm no longer in Chicago, community is part of my DNA. I seem to create it with others without trying.

It's almost like I can't help it. I'm still a pastor at heart, although I've been able to let go of many of the traditional roles of pastoring. I offer support where I can to others along the way, even though I do not actively seek to do so. My final words to the community before leaving were, "Whether I come back or not, I will do what I have always tried to do, to follow Jesus."

Today, I believe and am convinced that God is far more present in the details than is the devil. God has an incredible way of tying together the loose ends, or the ends that become loose, in ways like no other. I wish good for others, especially for the community that I labored in for so many years. Yes, I would do it again. Some of the greatest people I know live there. I look forward to being with them in heaven one day, but for now I love them from a distance.

I reflect often on the profound and prophetic conversation I had with my mother fifty years ago when she woke me at two a.m. to say, "You have nothing to offer to anyone."

My half-awake response was to simply agree. "You're right. I will have to learn."

And so I have. My witness to this day is that God is good. I now know Jesus in ways that I was not looking to know Him. I would not trade that knowledge for anything in the world.

The End

– Afterword –

Two years after completing the spiritual direction course at North Park Seminary, I had an onset of recurring dreams. In the dream, it was an ordinary day, but I was naked and unable to find my clothes. Others interacted with me normally, but I was conscious of my nakedness and searched desperately for my clothes. It was always a great relief to wake up and realize it wasn't real.

During my training, there was a presentation on dream interpretation. The process of interpretation was quite simple; the standout aspects of the dream were identified, then time was spent examining each aspect on its own separate from the oftentimes incongruence of the dream as a whole. In a way, it was an exercise of interior examination and became a creative way of having a devotion.

I contacted the presenter and was invited to attend a group meeting a few weeks later. When I shared my dream about being naked, I felt a kind of awkwardness from the other five or six gathered, who were all women. In reality, it may have only been my own inhibition around the subject of my dream. Some offered how this dream would make them feel, which helped me identify my feeling of being exposed. They asked if there was anything present in my life that made me feel this way.

There were many things, including Kirsten's battle

with addiction, which, at that time, was only growing worse. Most people in the community were kind to her when she visited, but there were some stares of disbelief from those who were shocked by her haunting appearance. Someone once offered, "I am sorry for your humiliation." That comment actually identified what I truly felt but had not given myself permission to name. I was also painfully aware of a dissonance I was feeling with some of the leaders in my community with whom I had served and been friends with for forty years. When Dawn passed, we faced a significant absence that forced us to address the matter of adding new leaders to our council of pastors. These conversations were tense as we all tried to envision how that would be done. I often felt like I was sitting in the crosshairs of others' resistance and scorn. The turmoil sat heavy with me. The saying "don't fix what isn't broken" was not applicable with our growing need for inclusion, just as it hadn't been applicable when we needed to change our cleaning routine after thirty years. Change was necessary in spite of the age-old adage that "all change is perceived as loss." The highly-charged disappointment I felt from some, combined with the weight of shame and fear I carried about my daughter and the sorrow of losing Dawn, left me feeling naked.

As I shared this, I remembered a rendition of the crucifixion I had seen in a presentation on the Stations of the Cross. The crucified Jesus hung on the cross naked. The drawing was not graphic, but clearly there wasn't a loin cloth on the body. Jesus hung there in utter humiliation for all to see. As I sat with this image and the reflections of my dream, I had a profound sense of being accompanied. Our group concluded with a moment of silence. Afterwards my dreams no longer occurred.

That was more than ten years ago. Then, as I finished writing this book, I had the dream again. When I awoke, I asked myself where I was presently feeling naked in life. While I don't have any regrets and am greatly blessed to live near Kirsten and her family and enjoy frequent visits from my daughter, Mindy, who lives in Chicago, I am aware that I live life brokenhearted in ways I never imagined. My story of life in my community has been taken away from me. The writing of this memoir has felt like a long exposé of my whole life. When I ponder the end of Jesus's life and the way he died in utter humiliation, I understand it in ways I never have before. He died brokenhearted for all humankind. Because of this, I believe He is near to those who are brokenhearted and desires to be with each of us in our sorrows.

We live in a world of unfixable things. I am intimately acquainted with these great unfixables from living life in community with hundreds of others. We shared a common vision and hope of becoming fixed and in turn helping fix others. But as hard as I have tried to realize this vision, I have come up short time and time again in my own life and with those I wanted to help. Spiritual direction has helped me to explore and experience life differently and adjust my perspective about what being fixed may look like. Spiritual direction encourages acceptance and acknowledgement of reality, something I, like others, often try to avoid. I believe prayer is the pursuit of finding that God is present, though it may appear to us first that He is absent. As someone aptly said, "Being present is not God's problem." That may be difficult to acknowledge, but moving forward, for me, has been about discovering the presence of God in the midst of my own brokenness and in the brokenness of others.

I am one of those for whom the Apostle Paul said, "Brothers and sisters, think of what you were when you were called. Not many of you were wise by human standards; not many were influential; not many were of noble birth" (1Cor.1:26). I've often said Jesus was scraping the bottom of the barrel to find me. It is fair to say that I've hardly done anything by myself and living in community with others shone a bright light on that truth. The one exception was that of choosing Christ, and even that decision was likely due to the influence of others throughout my life.

Please do not think I have succumbed to being a fatalist or a devoted pessimist. Hardly. I live in hope more today than ever. It is said hope grows in hopeless situations. I've lived through plenty of situations where I felt like I was hoping against hope. It is the soil in which I've thrived. But my hope now is that, by reading my life story, you may thrive in the midst of whatever unfixable situations you're facing and that you will discover, as I did, that you are not alone.

– Acknowledgments –

I have the utmost gratitude for my parents, Neil and Janice Taylor; my siblings and their spouses, Jan and Wayne Perpall and Mark and Ginny Taylor; my wife of forty-seven years, Pegge; my daughters, Mindy Taylor and Kirsten Packett and her husband, Tyler; my tireless grandson, Max; and the many people I have lived with in community over the past forty-five years. I believe myself to be filthy rich with friends.

I am indebted to those who have encouraged my writing, especially to my writing coach, Tammy Letherer, author of *The Buddha at My Table*, who has worked with me for more than a year to help bring shape to my story. Without Tammy, I'd still be lost in a forest of words stuck in the middle of quicksand.

If I were to make a list of everyone who has been important to me while writing, it would have to be another ten or twenty pages. But I'd be remiss not to mention a few by name. I am indebted to and grateful for Jane Hertenstein and Jon Trott, some of the first to read my writings, which were more similar to a crazy man's journal entries. I am grateful to my long-time friend Scott Ingerson, who some refer to as my favorite son, for his support in multiple ways over the past few years.

One of the Covenant Church's banners comes from Psalm 119:63. "I am a companion of all who fear you." I want to recognize some of the many companions of mine in the Covenant Church: Rev. Soong-Chan Rah, Rev. Jay Phelan, Rev. Glenn Palmberg, Rev. Paul E. Larson, Rev. Dawn and Andrew Burnett and the congregation at Celebration Covenant Church in Omaha, Nebraska, Rev. David Dillon, Rev. Steve Peterson, Rev. Paul de Neui, Rev. Donn Engebretson, and Rev. Curt Peterson. Father Lorn Snow of St. John's at Creighton University and Father Dennis Hanneman who have both lent me their ears when we meet for spiritual direction every month. John and Tina Herrin and Tom and Janet Cameron helped provide valuable decompression time with long weekends in a cabin on Lake Michigan. Rev. Ron Brown and Pastor Jym Kay exercised their gifts of encouragement. I must include Karl and Sarah Sullivan whom I hope to live next to in heaven. And last but not least, I thank Dave and Lois Jury. Sadly, Lois passed away in April 2020 from cancer. She and I enjoyed many difficult and open conversations before she departed life on earth. She often encouraged me by saying, "I would want to know the whole story."

If you have found something meaningful for yourself in my story, I'd love to hear from you!

Neil *(signed with Terry's pen)*

thegreatunfixables@gmail.com

– Postscript –

I have finished reading your book.

I loved your childhood stories. I laughed out loud at them, at forty years old, just like I did at the age of four and five. As your daughter, and with the memory of an elephant, I knew each line that would come in each story before even reading it.

The middle of the book is a bit of a horror story, as it should be. The stories of alcoholism and addiction are rarely described as anything but a nightmare for all involved. There are parts of my story described in your book that make me cringe and parts I felt were maybe described incorrectly. Then I realized that these were your feelings, your point of view, your experiences, and your recollections. So any of my thoughts or changes are not all that important. I told you early on in my sobriety that you were free to share my addiction story and your journey through it however you like, to bring you healing or benefit another. I was experiencing my own recovery and healing from my mess, and I wanted you to experience the same.

I can also say, with a bit of hesitation, that I would do it all again too. By that I mean that, if living my past differently would have an impact on my life presently, I would not do it differently. I am at peace with who I am (most days). I am clear in my decisions. I know when I have done wrong, and I know how to amend and make those wrongs right. I have you, Mom, Mindy, and so many of the friends I lost along the way who have found their way back into my life. I have been blessed to also build a family of my own. Today I am of sound mind, able body, and I have a joyful soul and heart of flesh, not of stone.

As I read the chapters on your unjust treatment and victimization by the ECC and by our own church family, I experienced or re-experienced the anger I felt for all those who acted horribly or stood by silently and complicit. I cried at your pain and heartbreak. I stayed with these feelings for a while in this section because that is what anger does. When anger, as strong as love, takes hold and is left unchecked, it can leave you reckless. I went to bed and had a terrible night's sleep. I woke the next day with Max's sweet little face directly in front of mine as he was hogging my pillow (per usual), and I realized I was ready to move on from the anger.

I picked up reading where I had left off. I was still outraged by the terrible mismanagement inflicted on you by so many of your peers within the ECC, and those in your own church community. As I read and learned of your decisions to move forward in forgiveness and love, I found myself knowing that if you could choose to do that, then so must I try.

I am proud and in awe of your bold honesty in this book. You wrote things and confessed to parts of your life's journey, thus far, that most people would not have the courage to talk about, let alone put down on paper, where once written, can't be taken back. There is an AA slogan that says, "Secrets keep you sick!"

I hope this book is your ultimate vaccine, curing you of

all that has ailed you since the beginning of this nightmare, and that it cures you of living through the nightmare with me.

Know this: you did not fail as a father! In fact, nothing could be farther from the truth. You were and are my greatest teacher and my strongest champion, through sickness and health.

I love you beyond words!

– Little Miss Nicole (aka Kirsten)

– Appendix –

Full text of my response to the Board of Ordered Ministry, (June, 2018) :

When Jesus People became a member church with the ECC in 1989, it provided for me as a pastor a place to broaden my companionship with others. I'm proud to say I have found many companions in the ECC. (Psalm 119:63). Because of this, it makes it difficult for me to express the disappointment I have with this board and the leadership of the ECC, for whom I have loved and held deep respect for. I believe myself to be one of ECC's strongest supporters.

The lack of exercising "due process" that resulted in my suspension one year ago has been an extremely painful and chaotic time for me, my wife, our adult daughters, and I believe for my community as well. The ECC did not receive a complaint from an outside source about me. Rather, I personally informed the executive minister, the Rev. Mark Novak, and Rev. Carol Lawson about allegations made against me of child molestation from a person who had been cared for by my wife and me forty years ago. My wife Pegge and I gave care to three children while their mother took time to gain stability in her own life and prepare to give birth to her fourth child. This woman lived with us in our community and had daily contact with her kids, while Pegge and I agreed to oversee the children's daily routines of getting to school on time, eating meals, assisting them with their homework, and trying to provide a stable home environment, as best we knew how. We were just beginning to start a family with our own children, but volunteered to help meet the needs of this woman and her children.

The irony of all this was my naiveté in thinking with the accusation against me as an ordained minister in the ECC, I would find additional support from my denomination. My life experience has now been discovering the opposite to be true. The five months prior to my suspension could have been spent in exercising "due process," but to my knowledge none was done. In fact, I believe no one has paid much attention to this until a recent phone call from Rev. Terry Marks asking my permission to contact my accuser in hopes of lifting my suspension. Contacting a person bringing such accusations against clergy should be part and parcel of exercising care for its clergy, and should not need mine or anyone's permission.

With a little investigation it would have been easy to discover a connection with former disgruntled members who have attacked our community over the years, dating back to when we first became a member church of the ECC. In the early 90s we were included in a book on abusive churches by an author who was eventually highly criticized by his own sociology contemporaries for his blatant lack of ethical methodology. Ten years later articles appeared for two days in a row on the front pages of the Chicago Tribune depicting what basically amounted to a church split. And now, ten years later, we find ourselves embroiled once again with a more insidious attack alleging us to be like the Catholic Church, deliberately covering over sex offenders and exposing children to further harm. These claims allege that all the children in our community were fair game for sexual exploitation by all the adult men in our community. If this were true then these claimants have unwittingly indicted their own fathers as child molesters, too. Eventually, the group of claimants became aware of the need to name an ordained minister from our leadership team at Jesus People in hopes of bolstering their claims of including the ECC. My observation over these past years has been that these claimants aggressively enlist whoever they can to make accusations in order to lend credence to their claims.

In times past, any and all allegations of these sorts were investigated responsibly by the ECC. In this matter with me, it feels like "duck and cover" was the action the ECC took. My concern and disappointment is and has been "Where is the Church?" Pastor Andrew Burnett said he remembers well when the Rev. Dave Kersten said to his class of ordinands, "If you get in trouble the ECC will take care of the church, and Jesus will take care of you." After the suspension was given to me over the phone by Rev. Mark Novak and a month later upheld by the Board of the Ministry at the 2017 Annual Meeting, I agreeably attended the Midwest Development Ministry for my own growth assessment in August. Since then I have not heard from anyone on the Board or from the leadership of the ECC until a month ago when I heard from Rev. Theresa Marks.

Fortunately, I am well practiced in self care. Being trained in spiritual direction has greatly assisted me to find the Presence of God through these horrific and difficult events. During this year I have participated in worship and bible study at Celebration Covenant Church in Omaha, where I moved to be near my daughter, grandson, and son-in-law. I meet monthly with a spiritual director who is a priest at Creighton University, and though I deliberately cut back my own practice of giving spiritual direction, I still meet as a director with a few Covenant Pastors online. One is in a province in Canada where there isn't any accessibility to a spiritual director. I also joined an "improv group" for my own personal therapy of doing something I am not comfortable doing. I have friends that I am in regular contact with, who call or write to check up on me.

Let me say I am in support of suspension over agreed standards set for the clergy of the ECC, but not without due process given first. This allegation against me came from someone who is an adult, who does not live in the Jesus People community and does not attend the Jesus People church service. I believe with a little effort, surely in the five months prior to my suspension, it could have been discovered that complaints of this nature and or the fantastical allegations made have ever previously been raised about me or my wife during our forty-five year history at Jesus People, where we both joined as teenagers.

Truthfully, my life will never be the same. This year long Sabbatical, as I've called it, in reality has been more like a year to ride out a tornadic storm. I believe Pegge and I will find our way forward in spite of what I see as a lack of responsible action in the way things have been handled. I've also seen and witnessed the providential love and care of God and know full well Jesus has taken care of me. Obviously, I am baffled and disappointed by the way all of this has transpired with the leadership of the ECC and the

Board of the Ordered Ministry. Only last week I had a phone call from a pastor with the ECC whose young daughter acted out with another young child her age. He called asking for my advice, sharing his fear of somehow things ending up turning on him as it did with me, and how that would affect his livelihood if something like that happens to him.

I believe the care being given to the larger church as a whole is a direct reflection of the care given to individuals, especially in regard to its clergy, by this board and the leadership of the ECC. I find this to be the example of Christ while on earth with His own disciples. The questions I now live with and face daily are: Where to from here? And, what does it look like if I am truly forgiving not only to my accusers, but my own church family as well?

Jean Vanier, a mentor for me when it comes to living life in community with others, said, "If a community ever reaches its height, its heart will be forgiveness." Part of the challenges of my journey over this past year and moving forward is discovering the help I need from Jesus to make my contribution towards this height.

In closing, I am asking that this board, along with the leadership of the ECC, do its investigation into allegations made towards its clergy. Obviously, some matters require immediate attention and action, but the idea of a Zero Tolerance Policy that advocates action before investigation is basically communicating guilty until proven innocent. This type of policy is highly criticized by many, including the American Psychological Association, citing its potential to be egregiously unfair, draconian, and ultimately providing little benefit. I now join rank with these critics from my own experience of being acted against without due *diligence and having suffered its consequences, in being uprooted and now having my reputation questioned.*

Sincerely,
Rev. Neil Taylor

"I remain confident of this:
I will see the goodness of the Lord in the
land of the living."

– Psalm 27:13

– About Atmosphere Press –

Atmosphere Press is an independent, full-service publisher for excellent books in all genres and for all audiences. Learn more about what we do at atmospherepress.com.

We encourage you to check out some of Atmosphere's latest releases, which are available at Amazon.com and via order from your local bookstore:

Out and Back: Essays on a Family in Motion, by Elizabeth Templeman

Just Be Honest, by Cindy Yates

Detour: Lose Your Way, Find Your Path, by S. Mariah Rose

Convergence: The Interconnection of Extraordinary Experiences, by Barbara Mango and Lynn Miller

Sacred Fool, by Nathan Dean Talamantez

My Place in the Spiral, by Rebecca Beardsall

My Eight Dads, by Mark Kirby

Vespers' Lament: Essays Culture Critique, Future Suffering, and Christian Salvation, by Brian Howard Luce

Without Her: Memoir of a Family, by Patsy Creedy

Emotional Liberation: Life Beyond Triggers and Trauma, by GuruMeher Khalsa

The Space Between Seconds, by NY Haynes

License to Learn: Elevating Discomfort in Service of Lifelong Learning, by Anna Switzer Ph.D.

One Warrior to Another: A Vietnam Combat Veteran's Reflection, by Richard Cleaves

Waking Up Marriage, by Bill O'Herron

An Ambiguous Grief, a memoir by Dominique Hunter

Between Each Step: A Married Couple's Thru Hike On New Zealand's Te Araroa, by Patrice La Vigne

Geometry of Fire, by Paul Warmbier

My Cemetery Friends: A Garden of Encounters at Mount Saint Mary in Queens, by Vincent J. Tomeo

– About the Cover –

I am indebted to Janet Cameron for creating an artistic rendition from a photograph of my grandson floating in a pool. While it may seem like a disconnect to the title, it has everything to do with the theme and my life's experience from birth until now as I near my seventh decade of living. Facing *the great unfixables* in my life has been a kind of childlike decision to surrender my cares into the hands of a God who cares about what I care about more than me. This intentional "letting go" is so well expressed in Denise Levertov's poem with the words –

> "... so would I learn to attain
> freefall, and float
> Into Creator Spirit's deep embrace,
> knowing no effort earns
> that all-surrounding grace."

Thanks to my longtime friend, Janet Cameron, who has inspired so many through her art and design, especially over the years with Cornerstone Magazine and REZ Band. I feel privileged to have her art for the cover of my book.

You can view more of her artwork at
janetcameronart.com.

– About the Author –

Neil Taylor, a native of Florida, lived in Chicago for forty-five years, during which time he served as co-pastor for Jesus People USA, one of the largest intentional Christian communities in the United States. He is ordained by the Evangelical Covenant Church and continued his education at the C. John Weborg Center for Spiritual Direction at North Park University. Taylor and his wife Pegge are now retired and live in Omaha, Nebraska near one of his two daughters, his son-in-law, and his grandson. He continues to volunteer at Celebration Covenant Church in Omaha.

Made in the USA
Monee, IL
27 February 2022

91863696R00135